OUT OF THE WOODS

EMBRACING YOUR TESTIMONY

Nicole Miles

WESTBOW
P R E S S®
A DIVISION OF THOMAS NELSON
& ZONDERVAN

This story is based on true events.
All names and locations have been changed to
protect the anonymity of those involved.

Scripture quotations are from The Holy Bible, English Standard
Version® (ESV®), copyright © 2001 by Crossway, a publishing ministry
of Good News Publishers. Used by permission. All rights reserved.

Scripture taken from the King James Version of the Bible.

Scripture is taken from GOD'S WORD®, © 1995 God's Word to the
Nations. Used by permission of Baker Publishing Group.

WestBow books may be ordered through booksellers or by contacting:

WestBow Press
A Division of Thomas Nelson & Zondervan
1663 Liberty Drive
Bloomington, IN 47403
www.westbowpress.com
1 (866) 928-1240

Because of the dynamic nature of the internet, any web addresses or
links contained in this book may have changed since publication and
may no longer be valid. The views expressed in this work are solely those
of the author and do not necessarily reflect the views of the publisher,
and the publisher hereby disclaims any responsibility for them.

Any people depicted in stock imagery provided by Thinkstock are
models, and such images are being used for illustrative purposes only.
Certain stock imagery © Thinkstock.

ISBN: 978-1-5127-2466-0 (sc)
ISBN: 978-1-5127-2465-3 (e)

Library of Congress Control Number: 2015921099

Print information available on the last page.

WestBow Press rev. date: 1/5/2016

To those who are afraid to tell their testimony

ACKNOWLEDGEMENTS

To all my friends and family that stood by me and encouraged me to write this book. There were often times when I wanted to give up, but it was you that stood in the gap. This would not have been possible without you.

INTRODUCTION

Many people, especially women, are ashamed of where God brought them from. The enemy (Satan) wants you to be ashamed and afraid, but God does not give us the spirit of fear, but of power and love and self-control (2 Timothy 1:7). In order to be released from your past, you must release your testimony. Once, your testimony is released, it no longer holds you bound like a prisoner in chains. When your chains have become unshackled you are now released to receive God in all His Glory.

You are able to embrace and experience God's love, Grace, Mercy, Blessings, Gifts, and Holiness, all of who He is. God wants you to experience and embrace all of Him, but the only way to get there is being able to embrace all of who you are. This includes embracing your past. When you are afraid of your past it keeps you from experiencing the amazing future God has waiting for you. You are missing out on so much in life because you are imprisoned by your history. You are to rest in the fact that God is sovereign.

Michelle used to concern herself with the acceptance of other, and whether or not she would still be accepted if they knew her past. Now she finally understand that she is not to be concerned about the acceptance of man, but the acceptance of Christ.

Everyone has a past and that includes you too. God brought you out of your past and into the presence of Salvation. You are no longer your past, but God is your future.

In 1 Timothy 1:15, Paul states that he was the chief of sinners. Michelle felt the same about her life. She thought that there was no way anyone could have done anything worse than she had. Many of you that will read this have made the same claim, or at least thought it. Just like Paul, God showed Michelle mercy in her ignorance. And the grace of our Lord was exceeding abundant with faith and love which is in Christ Jesus (1 Timothy 1:13-14).

On Paul's journey to Damascus, God spoke to him. This was Paul's conversion from darkness to light. Now as he went on his way, he approached Damascus, and suddenly a light from heaven shone around him (Acts 9:3). This is a journey we all have taken as God was transforming us from darkness to light. And now that we are in His light we can no longer allow the darkness to keep our light from shining.

Your past is not who you are, but it is a testimony to the goodness of God. In 2 Corinthians 5:17 Paul writes "Therefore, if anyone is in Christ, he is a new creation." We have been made new in Christ. Let go of the chains that bind you and declare that you are free.

Listen to God as Michelle tells her story, her conversion from being released from the imprisonment that is her past. It is my prayer, as you read Michelle's story, you will embrace you story and share it with others. Now I charge each of you to release the fear that Satan put upon you and embrace the power we now have in Christ Jesus.

CHAPTER ONE

I grew up the youngest of four sisters. As I entered into my teenage years there were many stipulations placed on me. My sisters had become mothers during their teenage years, children raising children, and my mother was determined not to allow the same thing to happen to me. I saw firsthand what having a child as a teenager was like. Being a teenage mother was definitely not what I wanted for myself, but I felt as if I was being punished for the mistakes of someone else. Instead of following their footsteps I decided to make steps of my own. I had dreams for my future that did not involve motherhood as a teen.

I grew up in Lexington, a small town in Tennessee, and there was nothing productive for a young girl to do. I knew I had to do things differently with my life than everyone else, or I would indeed end up in the same predicament as my sisters. In order to change this cycle I knew that there were no other options, except to leave Lexington. Two weeks after my high school graduation, I got on the bus to Atlanta, Georgia with no intentions of looking back.

Atlanta was the place to be. A huge city compared to where I was from. The streets were busy with traffic and everyone seemed to be in a rush. This was my first time away from home and I had never seen anything like Atlanta. I finally had my freedom and I exhaled as the winds of Atlanta brushed across my skin.

I no longer had everyone watching every step I took and monitoring everything I did. I was an adult, a grown woman, and no one could tell me what to do anymore. This was going to be the first day of the rest of my life.

I had found a job through some friends of mine and I couldn't wait to get started. When I arrived everyone was in such a hurry, busily working and running around the office doing important tasks. Just being there made me feel important.

My first stop at the new company was to the Human Resource office. I sat quietly waiting with anticipation before they called my name to start my in-processing procedures. I was given so much information that my brain was on overload. I knew nothing about withholdings and taxes. I sat there in hopes that the Human Resource Officer would not steer me in the wrong direction. I tried paying attention as much as I could, but I walked out with a brain full of information and had no idea what it all meant. I was so excited that I wasn't going to let all that paperwork get me down.

Once my in-processing was complete, I was rushed into a training class for the remainder of the day. It seemed as if there was no end in sight. The instructor went on and on all day about procedures and protocol. I was glad to know that the entire room was filled with new employees, which made me feel a little more comfortable. I had met some exciting new friends who were all about the party life. A life I knew nothing of, but I was intrigued.

All they seemed to do were talk about parting and the men in their lives. They seemed to have been much more mature than I was, especially when it came to men. I sat quietly as they talked about things I knew nothing of, but surely wanted to experience. In an effort to fit in with the crowd I just laughed and nodded as if I knew exactly what they were talking about. I was embarrassed to let anyone know just how inexperienced I was.

Growing up my mother had always warned me about the friends I chose. "Birds of a feather flock together", she would say. She would always tell me whom I could and could not be friends with. It was her way of protecting me from the "bad influences" as she called them. In my rebellious state I refused to listen. I wanted to make my own decisions and didn't understand why my mother needed to pick my friends. I was not like my friends, "I was different", I would say. I was soon about to find out just how different I was.

As I was leaving work one day I heard someone call out, "Michelle!" I turned and looked, but there was no one that stood out in the crowd. I continued on my way, and again I heard, "Michelle!" I stopped to see who it was. Stepping out from the crowd stood the most gorgeous man I had ever seen. Not realizing, I became flushed and a smile formed across my face that stretched from one ear to the other. Why was this man calling out my name, and how did he know my name?

"Hi, my name is Terrance", he said in a deep masculine voice. "Nice to meet you." I replied. "You already know my name, so what can I do for you, Terrance?" My heart began pounding, twice as fast, as a rush of adrenalin ran through my body. I took a quick examination of how breathtaking he was from head to toe. My eyes scrolled his shaved head as it shined under the sunlight, to his broad shoulders, and down to the shine of his shoes that complimented his size thirteen feet.

Terrance stood about six feet tall with the smoothest chocolate skin I'd ever seen. While looking into his eyes, as they sparkled under the sunlight, he said to me, "I think you are so beautiful, and I just had to meet you." He proceeded to ask me out to dinner for the next evening. I didn't want to seem overeager, so I replied, "yes" with a slight hesitation. As if I had something else to do. He was ecstatic when I agreed to go out with him. After getting his composure together, he informed me that he would pick me up at 7:00.

This was going to be my first date ever. With such inexperience in the area of dating, I didn't really know what to expect. My friends never did talk much about the dating aspect as they did sex.

I grew up in the church, but hadn't been since moving to Atlanta, and was taught that having sex before marriage was a sin. Perhaps what I learned wasn't all true. After all, how sinful could it be if everyone else was doing it? Having sex was part of dating according to my friends. I had only imagined what sex would be like based on conversations, and it was finally my turn to have my own experiences. I would no longer have to sit quietly while my friends talked about their experiences. I would finally have something to share.

I knew that the thoughts I were having were not Godly, but the more I thought about them the less I thought about God. No matter how much my thoughts consumed me, it did not take away the voice of my mother. I could hear her whispering in my ears, warning me of the dangers the laid ahead, but I did all I could to block it out. I was not going to allow God nor my mother to take me from this opportunity to be with Terrance.

Terrance was every girl's dream. He was the type of guy I always dreamed of marrying as I was growing up. Just as he was my dream, I wanted to be his dream as well. I wanted to make sure I made an impression when he saw me again. I spent all day getting ready, picking out my evening attire, doing my hair, and making sure I wore the perfect fragrance that would want him to be close to me the entire evening. Everything had to be perfect, not a strand of hair could be out of place.

The time had come and Terrance arrived at my apartment promptly, as all gentlemen should. He walked me out to his car, opened the door, and when he closed the car door the wind caught his cologne and it blew in like a soft wind. The aroma of his cologne was intoxicating. All I wanted to do was lay my head in the nook of his neck and breathe him in. As we prepared to drive off Jazz music began to play on the radio. Things were starting off just right and Terrance knew exactly what he was doing.

We pulled up to the restaurant and the waiter escorted us to our table. Before leaving the waiter took our drink order. I was so nervous that my hands began to shake and my knees began knocking against one another. I tried all I could to hide it, but the more I tried to hide it the more nervous I became. Terrance looked at me with his gorgeous smile and simultaneously my hands stopped shaking and knees stopped knocking against one another. His smile brought a sense of calmness to me and I began to relax.

The waiter soon returned with our drinks and proceeded to take our meal order. I had never been to such an expensive restaurant before and I had no idea what to order. Terrance recognized my hesitation and recommended an entree for me. As we waited on our meals we talked about so much. Terrance was so inquisitive about me to the extent that I didn't find out much about him. He sat there entranced as he listened intently as I spoke on and on about myself. Time had gotten away from us till it seemed we were the only ones left in the restaurant. The night was going so well that neither of us wanted it to end. Terrance finally paid the check and we left the restaurant walking hand in hand.

As Terrance was driving me home, he asked if I would like to go bowling the next day. I had only bowled once before and wasn't very good at it, but I agreed so that I could see him again. Oh! How I wanted to see him again. That evening had gone so perfectly that I could only image how much better it would be as we continued to get to know one another. The anticipation of seeing him again seemed more exciting than the time we had just spent with one another.

We pulled up in front of my apartment and Terrance got out and walked me to the door. The questions, "Will he or will he not kiss me?" began to consume my thought process and sent my stomach into somersaults. After all, the good night kiss is the catapult of any date. He turned to me and stated how great a time he had at dinner. I agreed as he leaned in slowly and softly kissed me goodnight.

I didn't run into Terrance at work the next day, but I knew I would see him later. I was so unfocused that when the instructors stood to teach the training class the information flew in the midst of the air and dissipated. I sat there replaying the events from the night before in my head. I tried to pay attention, but my thoughts were keened on Terrance and nothing that was said turned my attention away.

The work day had finally ended and I rushed home to get ready for my date with Terrance. This time I wasn't so nervous, but instead I was excited. Since we were bowling I figured it would be more relaxed, but I still needed to dress to impress. I wanted to make sure I had Terrance's devoted attention. I decided to wear tight fitted jeans that really hugged my size eight figure with a nice flowing blouse and heals. When Terrance arrived at my place he couldn't take his eyes off me. When he looked at me with his deep hazel eyes I wanted nothing more than to close the door and stay home with him for the evening.

When we arrived at the bowling alley it seemed really deserted. Terrance took my hand and led me inside. He was excited about bowling. Bowling was one of his favorite activities that he really enjoyed. So, we checked in and retrieved our lane for the night. As I was changing shoes Terrance took the liberty in picking out the bowling balls. Set to go, the game finally began and Terrance bowled like a pro. He was very impressive and he took the game very serious. He also took time with me and made sure I was enjoying myself.

Throughout the night he kept finding different ways to touch me, as if he was giving me bowling lessons. I didn't mind though. All I wanted was for him to touch me. As we sat beside one another he would always make a gesture and place his hands on mine or place his hand on my knee. I did my best to turn away his advances toward me, but the more I tried seemed to edge him on even the more.

I got up to take my turn on the lane, I grabbed the ball and took my stance. As my arm swayed back Terrance called my name. I turned and found him standing right in front of me. What was I to do now? He leaned in and kissed me on the cheek and held me tightly. It didn't matter that we were standing in the middle of a bowling alley. All that mattered was that Terrance and I were there together, in that moment, sharing a beautiful experience and I didn't want him to let me go.

After that night Terrance and I were inseparable. I consumed myself with him as if nothing else in life mattered. Dating Terrance was like nothing I had ever imagined, but everything I had always wanted. I wanted to give Terrance all of me and all of me I gave.

Terrance never pressured me to be intimate, but I wanted more. After taking me out one Friday night, he walked me to my door. Right before he leaned in to kiss me goodnight, I invited him in for coffee. As we entered through the door and walked into the living area, I offered Terrance a seat on the sofa as I went into the kitchen to prepare the coffee. While walking back into the living area I rushed over to Terrance. He knew exactly what my intentions were and he had no problem accepting my advances toward him.

The night placed me on the clouds and I never wanted to come down. Unexpectedly, Terrance leaned in toward me and said, "I love you." In that moment I released all fears and doubts. I knew I was his and he was mine, and nothing could take that away.

One afternoon, we were hanging out watching a movie, and Terrance turned off the television and said, "We needed to talk". I knew something was wrong when he spoke those words, so I braced myself for the worst. Terrance began to breathe heavy and became very clammy. The more he hesitated the more fearful I had became. Things between him and I had been going well and I couldn't imagine what he was about to say to me, but I knew it wasn't going to good.

"Michelle, I'm married," He explained. Immediately my heart sank into the pits of my stomach. After all the time we spent together the thought of him being married was unimaginable. Without speaking a word tears began flowing down the cheeks of my face. "Michelle, don't cry." He said. My wife and I are going through a divorce right now, but I need to go out of town for a few days to finalize the divorce." He explained.

I was furious with Terrance. I knew that fornication was wrong, but he turned me into an adulterer and that was worse. I tried to reason with myself despite the anger I had toward him. I asked him why he hadn't come forth and told me sooner. He explained how afraid he was and that he didn't want to ruin what we had. As angry as I was with Terrance, I was more afraid of losing him, so I hugged him and whispered in his ear, "I forgive you."

I was so happy with Terrance, and things between us were going great. I couldn't imagine myself without him. Although, he didn't tell me from the beginning at least he did tell me. After all he was getting a divorce. I buried my anger and gave him the space he needed to take care of his divorce and tried to deal with my emotions on my own.

The next day Terrance flew out to Oklahoma to finalize his divorce, and I went to work as if everything was okay. I waited by the phone for him to call and give me an update, but that day my phone never rang. We had talked to one another every day and today things were different. I felt like I had been shut out. I started having the worst thoughts about what was taking place in Oklahoma. Could he have reconciled with his wife and wanted nothing to do with me anymore?

I waited two days and still heard nothing from him. All my insecurities came pouring out like rushing waters. I went into full blown panic. I started calling his phone and leaving messages in hopes that he would call me back. What was truly going on? This was nothing like the Terrance I had been with for the past few months.

After a week had gone by I decided to go by his place to see if he had made it back into town. If Terrance was going to leave me he would have to tell me face to face. He was not going to shut me out. He was only supposed to have been gone for three days. If he had returned without calling me then he was going to have another issue to deal with.

There I was standing at the front door facing all my fears. Part of me was hoping that he wasn't there, but either way I had to find out. I knocked on the door once very softly and allowing enough time for someone to come to the door. After no one answered, I knocked a second time. The door opened and it was Terrance's roommate. "Is Terrance home?" I asked. The roommate escorted me to the living room and offered me a seat on the sofa. Then he went toward the back of the apartment without saying a word. I knew then that Terrance was home and I became enraged on the inside, but I tried to contain myself.

Terrance came from the back room with a huge smile on his face as if he was happy to see me. He just entered the room as if everything was okay. I immediately jumped up from my seat and asked him if we could talk in private. He and his roommate shared a suspicious look as we walked passed him and went outside. I couldn't imagine what excuse he was going to use for not returning any of my phone calls while he was away.

While outside Terrance reached for my hand, but I quickly pulled away. He then said, "Michelle, I do need to talk to you about something very important." He had a terrifying look upon his face. All I wanted to know was why he didn't return any of my calls, but it seemed as if Terrance had another conversation he needed to have.

He turned to me and said, "I'm sorry." At this point I had no idea what he was sorry about, but never did I think I was about to hear the next words that came from his mouth. "Michelle, I lied to you. When I told you I was going to Oklahoma to finalize my divorce, it wasn't the truth," He said. My heart began to sink as I asked, "Why did you lie, and why did you go to Oklahoma?" I asked. He took a deep breath and said, "I was engaged when I met you and I went to Oklahoma to get married." He began to confess everything to me as I stood there with tears flowing down my cheeks unable to speak a word.

Disgust began to fill the pit of my stomach and it made me sick. How could this man, whom I loved so much, betray me this way? What did I do to deserve the heartache that I was experiencing? He had been engaged to another woman for months and was planning a wedding the entire time we were together. The tears began to rain uncontrollably. My life was falling apart and Terrance was the reason.

He just stood there apologizing as if his apologies were going to magically make up for his betrayal. There was no excuse for what he had done to me, and I wasn't going to allow him to get away with no consequences. I had gotten the strength to turn to him and say, "While you were in Oklahoma getting married, I found out that you are going to be a father." Terrance planted his face in his hands not knowing what to say. "Did I hear you correctly?" he stated. "Yes, I'm pregnant and you're the father." Not only had he ruined my life, he had also ruined his new marriage lying to both of us for months.

Terrance thought he would be able to have his fun with me before he tied the knot with his wife. I was so angry that I couldn't stand the sight of Terrance and before he could even comment on my pregnancy, I did the only thing I had the strength to do, I got in my car and drove away never looking back again.

I spent weeks trying to make sense of what happened between Terrance and I. Single parenthood was not the life I dreamed of having for myself, but it was the life I was facing.

How could I have allowed this to happen? Why wasn't I more cautious? Why didn't I take heed to my mother's warning? It was too late to think about the how and why. I had to face my future and the future of my unborn child.

Freedom

The greek word for freedom is "eleutheria" meaning 1. the liberty to do or to omit things having no relationship to salvation 2. Fancied liberty (liberty to do as one pleases) 3. Living as we should not as we please. Let's not confuse Freedom with Independence and Liberty as they are sometimes viewed interchangeable.

Desiring freedom is a desirable attribute. What leads most people into destruction is the type of freedom you are desiring. Often time people view freedom as being able to do what you want, when you want, and how you want. In Michelle's immaturity, she viewed freedom exactly that way. She wanted to be on her own, responsible for only herself, and having to answer to no one. Yes, that is freedom, but freedom in its entity is much more than that. Michelle walked in the freedom of the world and not the freedom that God offered her.

The world offers freedom of self-expression. This freedom of expression has exposed the nation and encouraged people to be open about their sin, to be proud instead of having a repenting heart. It has allowed man to no longer hide his desires, but to express them freely. It has place society in danger with an increase in crime. There are those that are expressing themselves through violent acts of killings, rapes, child molestations, riots, and much more.

When experiencing this type of freedom, people are searching to find who they truly are. They have no idea who they are as a person and what they want to do in life. They began searching through other avenues for purpose. When living in the freedom of self-expression people are moved by how they feel, and have no sense of direction.

Man doesn't realize that you will always be confused about who you are when you're looking to the wrong source. Society has painted a picture of who we should be, but God has already told us in His word who we are. When you continue to look to the world and to the emotions of your flesh, you will never identify with who God created you to be.

Self-expression in itself is a worldly term as we are to express who Christ is and not who we want to be in ourselves. I understand that every person individually has different personalities and everyone's personality is expressed differently. Regardless of the difference in personality, the personality of the Christian believer takes on the connotation of the character of Jesus Christ.

Another type of freedom is freedom from authority. Men want to be ruled by their own desires. They do not want anyone telling them what to do. I know all of you have heard your parents say at one point or another these exact words, "If you live under my roof you're going to follow my rules." The moment those words are spoken is the very moment a child decides he can have his freedom away from the authority of his parents. The moment your parents spoke those words to you your brain began to work. You then began to say, "I can't wait to be grown and move out of this house."

No matter where you are in life you will always be governed by rules and laws that have been placed on you by those in authority. Whether you are at home under your parent's authority or living life on your own. You have rules of how to govern yourself in a public setting, rules of the highway, and you have laws that govern the nation. Inevitably, you are always govern by a higher authority.

Then you have Spiritual freedom or freedom in Christ. As Christians we should all desire this freedom. To have freedom in Christ is a form of freedom that leads to completeness in Christ. To be in Christ is to be complete in yourself. To know who you are is to know who Christ himself is. There is an oneness or likeness to Christ when you have spiritual freedom. We have a freedom from the authority and restraints of this world.

As Christians we are not governed by the world, but we are under the authority of a higher power, which is God himself. God has created boundaries in Christ to protect us from being enslaved to sin and to protect us from the snares of the enemy. It is for freedom that Christ has come.

> **Since, therefore the children share in flesh and blood, he himself likewise partook of the same things, that through death he might destroy the one who has the power of death, that is, the devil, and deliver all those who through fear of death were subject to lifelong slavery.**
> **Galatians 2:14-15 (ESV)**

Freedom outside of Christ leads to sin and destruction. Freedom outside of Christ never delivers on the liberties that man desires. This lie the enemy tells promises complete satisfaction. If only I can do the things I want to do, when I want to do them and how I want, and not have anyone telling me what to do would make my life so much better. If I had all those things I would finally have the freedom that I yearned for all my life. As Nancy DeMoss states in her book *Lies Women Believe*, this is a lie the enemy told Michelle and she believed it. Instead, I became enslaved to lust and fornication.

The enemy is crafty and you must be prepared for his coming. Michelle was being enslaved without even knowing what the enemy was doing behind the scene. She was his puppet and he was the master. It wasn't until the end of the play that she realized his authority over her. The enemy began his skillful plan by first allowing her to hear.

The enemy enticed Michelle when she began listening to her friends talk about what was happening sexually between them and their boyfriends. The more she listened to them the more interested she became in the matter. This is how Satan started his attack on Eve in the garden. Satan was able to get Eve to listen to him. When we allow ourselves to take part of conversations that dishonors God, we are unavoidably setting ourselves up for destruction. Once the enemy has found an opening and gains entry into the field he then has an opportunity for destruction.

After a person hears something that interests them, which is lust, they began to process what was heard and it then produce thoughts. Now you have the enemy affecting your hearing and your thoughts, meaning he has control of the brain function. The brain is the largest and most complex organ in the human body that communicates with the rest of the body. If the enemy filtrate the brain it now affects the heart, the function of your hands and feet, and the mouth.

Once the enemy has control of the body, through the brain, he then began to lure its host with the lust of the eyes. Michelle lusted over Terrance the moment she saw him. His appearance was appealing to her. Then her rationality was overtaken by what the flesh desired. She began to have what I call the 'David syndrome'. In 2 Samuel as David is walking on his roof top late at night he looks over and sees Bathsheba bathing. He found her very beautiful and began to lust after her.

Michelle began to imagine things happening between Terrance and her before she went on their first date. She imagined those things she heard her friends speak of in many conversations. Michelle imagined the physical intimacy. The more she imagined the physical; there arose the desire to have the actual physical intimacy that she imagined. Remember how I said the enemy is crafty.

Michelle and Terrance began dating and she instantly became enslaved. The sin of listening to ungodliness developed into lusting after ungodliness. It then manifested itself into the act of ungodliness, which was fornication. She had no freedom, not the freedom she desired. The freedom she desired promised her joy and happiness, but what she received was heartache and pain.

> **For you were called to freedom, brothers. Only do not use your freedom as an opportunity for the flesh, but through love serve on another.**
> **Galatians 5:13 (ESV)**

Michelle got caught up in being free from the stigma that was placed on her, as a result of her sisters' behavior, not realizing that she wanted to do the very thing they were doing the entire time. She wanted the freedom to have boyfriends, go out to parties, and have sex if she so desired. Have you ever told your parents, "Just because it happened to them doesn't mean it would happen to me"? This was Michelle's statement every time she was denied her freedom to gratify the flesh.

Her mother was not denying her freedom. She was offering her protecting from destruction that would inevitably enslave her to the enemy of God, which is Satan. Michelle's mother was doing the very thing God is doing for us. Christ came to free us from the sins of this world by conquering it. Through the death of Christ we have been set free to live a life of freedom in Christ and to no longer be imprisoned by sin.

> In the same way we also, when we were children,
> were enslaved to the elementary principles of
> the world. But when the fullness of time had
> come, God sent forth his Son, born of Woman,
> born under the law, to redeem those who were
> under the law, so that we might receive adoption
> as sons. And because you are sons, God has sent
> the Spirit of his Son into our hearts, crying,
> "Abba! Father!" So you are no longer a slave, but
> a son, and if a son, then an heir through God.
>
> Galatians 4:3-7 (ESV)

There is so much freedom and liberty when living in Christ. Unlike the false promises the enemy gives, being liberated in Christ means being forgiven of our sins, having love, hope, joy, and eternal life through the shed blood of Jesus Christ. Christ has become our Cornerstone. Through His blood he has joined us together with God. True freedom comes from being united as one with God through obedience.

> If you keep my commandments, you will abide
> in my love, just as I have kept my Father's
> commandments and abide in his love.
>
> John 15:10 (ESV)

We all desire freedom, but as Christians, live your freedom in Christ. The freedom that is offered from this world comes at a high cost and that cost may be your life.

FREEDOM

There is much to be said about freedom,
to no longer be constrained or chained.
Set free to do whatever I desired to
do: to be the she I wanted to
There was an inner desire fighting to get out,
To run, dance, and prance all about.
This freedom kept calling my name,
and my freedom I would proclaim.
Freedom came with a price for me,
And the price almost took my life.

Freedom promised me all my desires,
to have joy and laughter,
and my happily ever after.
Freedom promised me to be whom I aspired to see.
Freedom told me all I wanted to hear,
Whispering all the sweet nothings in my ear.
This freedom came at a price for me,
And this price almost took my life.

A woman is not reduced to lying on her back.
I had dreams that filled a night sack.
Freedom went against all that I heard,
But what did they know? It was my time to run the show.
It was only me traveling this road,
And I would walk in rain, hail, or snow
To make sure it was my name being
called during the encore.
This freedom came at a price for me,
And the price almost took my life.

What freedom steals your essence, your
innocence, of who you are?
Freedom was disguised in mask of
brown skin and a deep voice.
It lied, killed, and destroyed.
The me I was and the me I tried to be.
My freedom came at a price for me,
And the price almost took my life.

CHAPTER TWO

Being an adult and out on my own was not what I thought it would be. Freedom came with a price. Not only was I dealing with heartbreak, I was dealing with single parenthood. I had no idea how I was going to raise a child on my own. I was scared and afraid of what would become of my future. I was faced with lots of decisions and I was not sure about any of them.

I was ashamed to tell anyone about my pregnancy, but it wasn't going to be long before I had no choice in the matter. I spent many nights crying into my pillow dealing with the guilt and shame of what I had done. I needed help and so I turned to the only person I knew that could help me, my mother.

I picked up the phone to call her and as the phone began to ring my entire body quivered in fear. Before she could answer the phone I heard her voice warning me against premarital sex and having children out of wedlock. I should have listened, but now it was too late. The moment she picked up the phone, she had already known something was bothering me. "Michelle, are you alright? You have constantly been on my mind. I've been worried about you." she said.

My mother seemed to know things before they even happened. She seemed to have had a sixth sense about things concerning her children. I couldn't hold back any longer and I began to cry out. Tears began to emerge uncontrollably. "Terrance and I broke up mom", I said. My mother was heartbroken for me. She hated to see me unhappy. She wanted to know what happened between us and so I told her everything. I had to build up the courage to tell my mother that I was having premarital sex. As hard as it was I knew the only way to get help was to confess. I knew my mom would be furious, but I had no other choice. "Michelle, how could you have let this happen?" she said, as her words echoed through the telephone. I could hear the disappointment in her voice. She knew I wasn't ready to be on my own, but she also knew she couldn't keep me at home forever.

My mother always believed I was an innocent girl and there was nothing that would make her believe anything differently. She could not imagine anyone defiling my innocence. Now her little girl was about to give birth to her own child and there was no denying my impurities now. It was a truth that my mother had to deal with and she could no longer live in denial.

I had finally accepted the reality of what was happening in my life. I began scheduling doctor appointments and after that it wasn't long before I became excited about becoming a mother. The fear of knowing that I was going into this situation alone was never far from my thoughts. I had my mother, but she was states away. I was on my own and I knew it would be difficult, but I believed that determination could take me far.

During my fifth month of pregnancy, the company I worked for received a new transfer from New York. His name was Jonathan, and I thought he was so adorable. He had such an innocent way about him. He was not what I would have considered my type at the time, but there was something about him that drew me in. I knew I couldn't go after him, being that I was pregnant, but I still had my imagination.

I was on my way to work one day and I spotted Jonathan walking to the office. In an effort to be nice I pulled over and offered him a ride. Not knowing who I was, he was hesitant, but he accepted the ride. We didn't have much to say to one another besides the normal greeting, but after a few minutes of silence Jonathan began to explain how he had just moved to Atlanta and didn't know anyone. I extended my hand of friendship and said, "If there is anything you need help with just let me know".

Giving Jonathan a ride to work became a regular occurrence. Whenever we were together it seemed like the longest ride to nowhere. Jonathan was a man of few words. He never spoke out of place, but was always cordial and respectful.

One evening there was a knock at the door. I wasn't expecting any visitors, but I went to the door to see who was there. To my surprise it was Jonathan. "I'm sorry to show up unannounced," he said, "but I wanted to show my appreciation for all your help by inviting you up stairs to have dinner and watch a movie with me." His offer caught me by surprise, but I was intrigued and accepted his invitation.

I wasn't sure if he was flirting with me or he genuinely wanted to say thank you. He and I never spoke of me being pregnant, but surely he knew. Anyone could look at me and clearly tell I was carrying a child. Did Jonathan not know or did he not care? I was too afraid to ask. I told Jonathan that I would meet him upstairs once I had gotten dressed.

When I arrived I noticed he had ordered some take out and rented quite a few movies. "I didn't know what kind of movie you liked, so I rented a movie from each movie genre." he said in such a sophisticated manner. I was impressed. He escorted me over to the sofa where he created a relaxed environment for us to eat and watch movies at the same time.

While watching the movies I kept looking over at him trying to figure him out, but I was getting nowhere. We sat there watching movie after movie. One movie became two, then three until we had watched them all.

After the last movie he asked if I wanted to go out and rent more movies and get more food. I agreed, as I had nothing else to do. So, we headed out to the movie rental store. As we walked around the store we discussed all the different movies that we had liked and seen before. I thought to myself, clearly he must be interested in me, but I was going to wait until he made the first move.

We stayed up watching movies and eating all night and before I knew it I had fallen asleep. Jonathan wrapped me in a blanket before falling asleep behind me on the sofa. He was very respectful and never tried to make a move on me. When I awakened the next morning I went downstairs to my place to get cleaned up and as soon as I jumped out of the shower Jonathan was knocking on the door asking me out for breakfast.

At this point I had no doubt he was interested in me, but I couldn't figure out why. While at breakfast Jonathan sat across from me just watching me eat as he slowly took bites of his food. Eventually, I finally asked what was going on. His response was, "I just like hanging out with you. I don't know anyone here and you seem pretty cool." So maybe that was just it. Maybe he was not interested in me, but was just lonely and wanted someone to hang out with.

Jonathan and I spent the entire weekend together. Not once did he try to lean in for a kiss or try to hold my hand.

We just had great conversation and enjoyed being in the company of one another. We talked as if we had known each other a lifetime. That was until we took in another movie, *The Best Man.*

The movie was coming to an end. The room was silent and I tried to hide the fact that this movie had brought tears to my eyes. As the movie was ending Taye Diggs proposed to Sanaa Lathan, and Jonathan turned to me and said, "I wish my whole life could be like this moment." What was this man saying to me? He could tell by the look on my face that I was confused. Then he turned and said, "Michelle, will you marry me?"

I was confused and excited all at the same time. I couldn't believe it. I didn't know if he was for real or was he joking. I had only known this guy for a few weeks, and this was our first time hanging out with each other. I began to quickly contemplate my current situation. I am a single mother about to give birth to a son and I do not want to raise this child alone. If I accept his proposal then I will no longer have to face single parenthood, but if I turn down this proposal then we could just remain friends. Before I could answer him, I needed to make sure he knew about my current situation.

I turned to him and said, "Jonathan, you do know I'm pregnant right?" He smiled and said, "Yes, and I think pregnancy is so beautiful." I couldn't believe it. He leaned over, placed his hand on my abdomen, and gently began to rub in a circular motion. I was astonished as I watched him in the moment. He seemed so gentle and caring. I thought to myself that I would never find another man like Jonathan. If I didn't accept his proposal I would never get the chance again. So, I smiled and said, "Yes!"

Jonathan was so happy. We embraced one another for the first time and shared our first kiss. He was gentle as he held me in his arm. We held the embrace for quite a while, neither of us wanted to let the other person go. I knew I had to tell him about Terrance. So, I pulled away and began to explain my situation further. Jonathan then gently sat his hand on my stomach again and declared that the child I was carrying would be his child. Jonathan was not concerned with my past and in that moment I knew that I had made the right decision.

Jonathan's parents were coming to town to visit and he couldn't wait for them to meet me. He told me all about them and his life growing up in New York. I couldn't wait to meet them. What I didn't know is that Jonathan hadn't told them anything about me. He reassured me that when they arrived he would sit them down and tell them the good news.

The day had come and Jonathan's parents had arrived in Atlanta. He took them straight to his apartment. This was the time he would tell them everything and I would soon be meeting my future in-laws. He had been gone for over an hour and then suddenly there was a knock at the door. When I came to the door Jonathan was standing there with a somber look on his face. "What's wrong?" I asked. He asked if he could come in and talk. At this point I became very nervous and concerned; I didn't know what was going on. Jonathan looked at me and said that his parents would not be coming down to meet me. When those words came out I immediately knew why they refused to meet me. Jonathan had told them about me being pregnant. "Michelle, there is more." He said. I couldn't imagine what else he was going to say. "We can't get married either." I was furious. "Why?" I asked. He sat and told me the conversation he had with his parents.

Jonathan's parents disapproved of their son marrying a pregnant woman. They questioned whether or not the child was his, but when they found out it wasn't they could not give him their blessing. I understood where they were coming from. They didn't want their son having the responsibility of raising another man's child and all the drama that would come along with that. I could not fault them for feeling the way they felt, but I didn't understand why Jonathan could no longer see me again. At the word of his parents he was abandoning me.

Perhaps, this was my punishment for saying yes; I accepted the proposal for all the wrong reasons, I didn't want to be a single mother. After trying to be reasonable I became angry. I was upset with Jonathan's parents for taking away a father for my child. I was trounced back into single parenthood instantly. I tried talking Jonathan out of his decision by trying to give him plenty of reasons to stay, but how could I force him to go against his parents?

After Jonathan's parents left town, Jonathan came by the apartment to check on me and see how I was doing. He apologized for being a jerk to me and asked me to forgive him. It was hard to forgive him, but I missed him so much. Jonathan fell to his knees and hugged me at the waist, and told me he loved me. As I looked into his eyes he asked me to marry him again, and again I said "yes". Four months later we were married.

A week after being married our son was born. Jonathan was instantly a father and was happier than I had ever seen him. Jonathan would not let our son out of his sight from the moment he was born. Jonathan truly embraced him as his own and immediately fell in love with him the same way he fell in love with me. We were now a family, a complete family and no one could interfere with that, not even Jonathan's parents.

I hadn't heard anything from Terrance once I told him I was pregnant. Apparently, he had been keeping track of me through mutual friends of ours. Through them he found out I had given birth. Terrance never came up to the hospital, but he called the hospital consistently until he finally got me on the phone. I spoke to him as Jonathan sat at the end of the hospital bed holding our son. Terrance didn't want to talk about the baby. He didn't seem concerned about him at all. He wanted to talk about the past, but to me the past was over. I was with Jonathan now.

When my son and I left the hospital Terrance began calling me at home. He wanted to get back together. I tried telling him I was married, but it didn't seem to matter to him. He told me that he finally told his wife about us and the baby. His wife didn't take the news well and immediately left him and filed for divorce. I couldn't feel sorry for him after how he had treated me. He was getting exactly what he deserved. I told Terrance that my son was no longer his child and that Jonathan was his father. Terrance hung up the phone and I never heard from him again.

Life with Jonathan was going great. Jonathan's position at the company was relocating him to California. It was an exciting time for us. With so many changes, Jonathan and I decided that I should stay home and raise our son, and so I put in my two week notice at work and prepared our family to leave for California. I was pleased to stay home and take care of the family. Everything was falling into place just the way I want and I didn't believe life could get any better.

I hadn't been to church since I left home, but I wanted to raise my son up in the church just as my parents did me. I had promised God long ago that when He blessed me with a child, I would make sure that my child would know who He was. Jonathan was not a religious person, but he wanted to make me happy. So after arriving in California he found us a church to attend. It took a few months, but we finally settled at Bythway Baptist Church.

Bythway reminded me so much of the church I grew up in. I loved singing those old Baptist Hymns and hearing the Pastor preached the Words of God as sweat spewed from his forehead. Soon after arriving Jonathan confessed Christ as his Lord and Savior and was baptized. After being up on the mountain top I knew I had nowhere else to go, but down.

A few months later Jonathan started working long hours. Some days we didn't see each other until late at night, if we saw each other at all. I started having insecurities about the relationship. With me being at home alone with the baby and Jonathan always working, I had plenty of time to imagine the worst. I was questioning Jonathan's love for me and whether or not he was being faithful during those long hours he worked.

Every time I saw Jonathan I was trying to get him to reassure me that everything was okay with us. He became very frustrated with me for asking him all the time if he still loved me. While I was questioning his love for me Jonathan had insecurities of his own. He knew I wasn't pleased with him working all the time and so he questioned my love for him. My time at home became lonelier with each passing day, and with each passing day my mind began to imagine the worst. I had to find something to do to get my mind back on the right track.

I spoke with Jonathan about the possibility of me going back to work, but he didn't seem to like the idea at first. He really didn't want me putting our son in child care with strangers looking after him. I understood at the time, but yet there was a lack of fulfillment in my life. I became very dissatisfied and unfulfilled in the marriage. I felt as if there was something I was missing outside of being a wife and mother. I didn't understand how the joy I felt months earlier had turned into a battle of love. I couldn't figure it out. Jonathan worshiped me, how could I question that. He had given me all any woman could ever ask for.

Faith & Waiting

One of the things that I have seen many Christians struggle with is having faith and waiting on God. People often put their faith in the wrong things. Their faith is placed on themselves, other people, money, and material things. This is what I like to call misplaced faith.

Now faith is the assurance of things hoped for, the conviction of things not seen.
Hebrew 11:1 (ESV)

When life has dealt us a bad hand the discontentment destroys our faith in life. The same thing can be said when we put our faith in family and friends. When they disappoint us, by not fulfilling the need in our lives, we lose faith in man. This is because we have misplaced our faith.

As we looked back over the events of Michelle's life so far, you can see that she had lost all faith. Not because God disappointed her, but because her faith was in Terrance and he disappointed her. She did not want to wait on God nor did she have enough Faith to trust that He would work things out. All she knew was that she did not want to be a single mother and any opportunity that came her way would be acceptable if it kept her from raising a child on her own.

Hope deferred makes the heart sick, but a desire fulfilled is a tree of life.
Proverbs 13:12 (ESV)

All the hopes and dreams Michelle desired for her life were now deferred. They were ultimately destroyed the moment she became pregnant. She thought having a baby was the end of her life. The moment Jonathan and Michelle became married she figured that her dreams, ultimately her life, had been restored. Her faith turned from Terrance and repositioned itself to Jonathan. The enemy has a way of turning your eyes away from God and placing hindrances before you that will keep your faith misplaced.

In order to get what we want and need from God it is in the waiting. Waiting on God means that God is the author and finisher over our lives, He is Lord. If we as Christians are not willing to wait on God, it is ultimately saying that God cannot do what He has promised in his word.

Waiting on God also demonstrates our faith to the world that God can do and will do far greater than any man could. When we decide to take charge of our lives or take precedent over God we are ultimately telling God that we do not need Him. What a tragedy to not need God.

Michelle's faith was not in God. She sought after her own desires. She sought after Terrance and then sought after marriage. Michelle believed that she alone had the ability to fix the situation when the opportunity presented itself. She didn't need God. She believed that if she married Jonathan it would eradicate the position she was facing. She didn't have faith that God could sustain her in her present situation, but being with Jonathan would be the solution.

There is not a more patient being than God himself. As I studied the book of Jeremiah, I realized just how patient God is with His people. Even when we are in sin, God waits patiently for us to return. God waited forty years for Israel and Judah to turn from their sin. Judah's sin was not without consequence, but yet God waited. God sent Jeremiah, on more than one occasion, to warn them that if they did not repent that God will allow them to be overtaken by their enemies.

God's people did not have faith that god would send Babylon to overtake them, but in the end God followed through on His word.

As Christian, no matter what we are going through, we must have faith and wait on God. He will see us through no matter what the situation may be. There is no situation that God cannot handle.

Not trusting God leads us to hopelessness and desperation. Michelle did not fall on her knees and ask God for help or forgiveness. She went from acknowledging her pregnancy, being heartbroken by the one she loved, and then plummeted into desperation.

In Isaiah 38 Hezekiah could have fallen into complete desperation when Isaiah the prophet told him of his imminent death, but instead of turning away from God he went before God. Hezekiah didn't panic nor did he become desperate. He went before God and asked God to remember him.

> **In those days Hezekiah became sick and was about to die. The Prophet Isaiah son of Amoz, came to him and said, "This is what the Lord says: Give final instructions to your household, because you're about to die. You won't get well." Hezekiah turned to the wall and prayed to the Lord. "Please, Lord, remember how I've lived faithfully and sincerely in your presence. I've done what you consider right." And he cried bitterly.**
>
> **Isaiah 38:1-3 (GWT)**

When we are in a situation that causes turmoil in our lives the first reactions is to panic. As Christians we learn to handle our situations differently than we did when we were in the world. We should follow the example of Hezekiah and pray to God. God is our sustainer and going before Him shows that He is the authority in our lives. God's plan for our lives is perfect. God will never do harm to His people. You may not understand it as you are going through, but there is a purpose for your "going through".

> **For I know the plans I have for you, declares the Lord, plans for welfare and not for evil, to give you a future and a hope.**
> **Jeremiah 29:11 (ESV)**

When Michelle found out she was pregnant she tried to envision what her life would be like in the future, as if she had that ability, but all she could see was a life of struggles and suffering. She did not take into consideration that God is the giver and sustainer of life. Her child was not a tragedy, but not trusting and waiting on God was the tragedy. By turning to Jonathan as her solution she was ultimately rejecting God and His plan by developing her own plan.

Whenever you are in a situation, by your own hands (sin) or through test and trials, fall on your knees before God and seek His guidance. Hezekiah trusted God and his faith was rewarded.

> **Then the Lord spoke his word to Isaiah, "Go and say to Hezekiah, 'This is what the Lord God of your ancestor David says: I've heard your prayer. I've seen your tears. I'm going to give you 15 more years to live.**
> **Isaiah 38:4-5 (GWT)**

I've heard the term blind faith used on many occasions in my life. What God describes as faith is not what the world calls blind faith. Blind faith is when you believe in something without having an understanding nor being able to conceive it. The faith we have in God is dependent on who we know Him to be.

> **God is not a man, that he should lie, or a son of man, that he should change his mind. Has He said, and will he not do it? Or has he spoken, and will he not fulfill it?**
>
> **Numbers 23:19 (ESV)**

Despite where you are in life, God will make a way. He promised to never leave us nor forsake us. Even in our mess ups, you must walk in faith. Not knowing what God will do, but having faith that he will forgive you and see you through. This is not permission to continue in sin, but an opportunity to run to the Throne of Grace and repent.

> **They that wait on the Lord shall renew their strength; they shall mount up with wings like eagles; they shall run and not be weary; they shall walk and not faint.**
>
> **Isaiah 30:31 (ESV)**

WAIT ON GOD!

SWEETNESS

Sweetness fell like morning dew,
Adding beauty to all it touched.
Worries vanished as the sweetness melted
like snow on a winter's day.
How can I help you?
Sweetness asked.
Take away the rain that caused all my pain
And let the drops drain away.

Sweetness fell like morning dew
and brought sunshine when clouds were blue.
A storm is brewing,
The wind is swaying,
and lighting seems to be breaking loose.

Sweetness fell like the morning dew,
to open my eyes,
to say "I love you".
Sweetness came to wipe away all my sadness
and birth radiance and gladness.
Sweetness fell like morning dew
Sweetness, I love you too.

CHAPTER THREE

It was New Year's Eve during our Annual Watch Night Service at Bythway Baptist that my eyes set on Kendrick. Kendrick was the Pastor of the Bythway Baptist Church where Jonathan and I attended. I watched Kendrick as he preached his New Year's Eve sermon with such love and admiration for God. As he preached I suddenly noticed how my thoughts shifted. Instead of paying attention to what God was saying, I paid closer attention to the man. Lust began to pour over me.

Kendrick stood about 6'2" tall, slender, brown skinned, and to top it off he had a wonderful singing voice. It seemed as if when he preached his words came out like music. It was something beautiful to behold. My thoughts of him seem to just take over at that very moment. With every word he spoke my lust grew stronger and stronger, almost unattainable. I sat there squirming in my seat, crossing and uncrossing my legs. He began to get deep into his sermon, like most Baptist preachers do, and he began to scream and belch out the Word of Truth. When he screamed I screamed on the inside. When he began to dance, I began to imagine him dancing with me. My thoughts had completely taken me away.

As Jonathan and I began to drive home after service, I began to look at Jonathan and think of all the things I wanted so much to change about him. All the ways he and Kendrick were different. It did not matter whether my thoughts about Jonathan were true or not. It was how I had imagined him in the moment. I wanted to fulfill my desire for Kendrick and Jonathan was an obstacle that was currently in the way.

The more I thought about Kendrick the more I found fault in Jonathan. Jonathan was my savior from being a single parent, but I still wanted to explore. Kendrick would be my adventure while Jonathan would have my love. I knew eventually the opportunity would present itself with Kendrick if only I could get close enough to him.

During Bible Studies I would ask lots of questions to try to get him to notice me. When I would inquire about biblical things it seemed to bring joy to his eyes. He enjoyed teaching and the more inquisitive the church members were the more he enjoyed it.

Later, I found out that Kendrick was the Sunday School teacher for the Adult Class at the church. Jonathan and I never attended Sunday School after we became members of Bythway Baptist, but I thought this would be another chance to get Kendrick to notice me more. I spoke with Jonathan about my desire to start going to Sunday School. Anything concerning the church Jonathan always said yes.

During Sunday School I would always sit up front, when I attended alone. Jonathan would stay home often times with our son during that time until it was time for church service. I could never seem to get an opportunity to talk with Kendrick one on one, until a few weeks later my phone rang.

I couldn't believe it. Kendrick was calling my house asking for me. I was astonished and excited at the same time. I tried to hide my excitement, braced myself and answered, "How are you today Pastor?" He responded by saying he was fine, but needed my help.

He told me that his current Secretary would be moving and that he was looking for someone to replace her. "Sister Smith, I thought about you." He said. I was thrilled to know that I was not far from his thoughts. "Are you interested in taking the position?" he asked. Without hesitation I leaped at the opportunity. Kendrick was pleased with my decision to accept the position. This was going to be my chance to get close enough to him so that I would be able to finally make my move.

My thoughts once again took over me and my lust grew stronger knowing that we would be working close together. I started thinking about all the long days and hours we would have alone, and all the opportunities I would have to seduce him.

Kendrick scheduled a meeting for me to come by the church to pick up all the necessary files and manuals I would need for the new position. I could not wait to see him again. I frolicked around the house for days excited about my meeting with him. My plan was coming together and I was just a step closer to getting what I desired.

The day had finally arrived for me to meet with Kendrick. I arrived with such excitement, but my excitement soon dissipated when I walked through the door and saw Kendrick's wife seated next to him in his office. I was disappointed when I saw his wife, but I tried to hide the disappointment on my face as I greeted the two of them. Although, I was not going to be able to say anything to Kendrick that day, I knew my time would come again. I knew Kendrick was married, but I had no thoughts or concerns about her.

Tammy, Kendrick's wife, greeted me with such warmth and excitement. She was a very nice lady, but I was not going to let her get in the way of my plans. She gestured for me to have a seat and so I did. They both went over all the documents and the uses for each one. I sat as if I was intensely listening while a dragon fire was raging on the inside. I planned my next opportunity in my head and this time Tammy was not going to be around.

A few weeks later, during a bible study, Kendrick announced that he would be visiting all the members of the church to get ideas on how to improve the service. He stated that he would be contacting each of us to schedule a day and time to come by. Knowing that Kendrick would be coming by the house excited me.

I spent the next few days coming up with questions and ideas, so that we would have something to discuss during our meeting. I didn't want to seem unprepared, therefore I made sure I was ready. I cared about the church, but I wanted to impress Kendrick more. The church was important to him and I needed it to be important to me too.

Later, in the same week, Kendrick got word that he was going to have to leave the country for a few months. This was devastating news to me. This was becoming a disappointment. Every time I thought I would be getting my opportunity with Kendrick something always seemed to happen. I didn't know what I was going to do all those months he would be away, but I was already anticipating his return.

After Kendrick left the next week we spoke frequently to discuss church business. With every conversation we had with one another seemed to become longer each time. After a while we began carrying causal conversation that was no longer about church business. We spoke about life, family, and careers as if we were really trying to get to know one another. In all of our conversations we never spoke of our spouses. I felt close to him after having so many conversations. During this time everything between Kendrick and I were still innocent, except my thoughts, but getting to know him better made me feel more comfortable in making my next move.

Then one day Kendrick called, as he would normally do, and surprised me by letting me know that he would be returning sooner than expected. This was great news to me. I couldn't wait to see him. The few weeks that had passed by without seeing him seemed like an eternity.

As soon as Kendrick arrived home he scheduled his meeting with all the families of the church. Jonathan scheduled our meeting after work hours so that he would be available to attend. Although, Jonathan would be present I didn't allow that to minimize the joy I had to see Kendrick. I just needed to set my eyes on him and I would feel better.

The day had finally arrived for my family to meet with Kendrick. I spent the entire day preparing. I went to the super market to purchase refreshments, cleaned the house, and made sure everything was in order. Once, I finished running errands, I picked out my attire to wear. I had to think carefully about my clothing choice. I wanted Kendrick to notice me, but I needed to make sure that Jonathan would not get suspicious. After I had finally completed all my tasks, I lit candles throughout the house to create a warm and welcoming environment.

Jonathan called home half an hour before our scheduled meeting with Kendrick to let me know that he was not going to be able to make it home in time. Jonathan seemed very disappointed, but I was thrilled. I tried hiding my excitement as I spoke with him on the phone. "I understand." I said. Before we ended our conversation, Jonathan wanted to let me know of suggestions he wanted me to mention to Kendrick.

Kendrick arrived promptly, as I knew he would. I answered the door, with a huge smile on my face, and greeted him. I proceeded and directed Kendrick to the living room area to be seated. All of a sudden I became so nervous. I offered him something to drink and an open invitation to the refreshments that were on the coffee table.

Kendrick noticed that Jonathan had not come out to greet him and so he inquired of his whereabouts. I informed him that my husband had called and would be working late, but that it was okay for us to conduct the meeting alone. Kendrick didn't seem to have an issue, and so we proceeded with the meeting.

Kendrick began discussing with me what he and other church members had already discussed, but I couldn't focus. My mind kept wondering about unsavory things, but then finally he asked for my opinion. I went ahead and mentioned those things Jonathan asked me to inquire about. All the other suggestion and comments were the same as what other members had already discussed with him.

An opportunity presented itself for me to interrupt and switch the subject. "Pastor, what advice do you give to someone that is having inappropriate feelings for another member of the church?" I said. I could tell by the look on his face that the question threw him off guard and he didn't know how to respond. I focused intently to see what his response would be. At a loss for words and a bit confused, he leaned forward on the sofa, as his long legs bent toward his chest, in deep thought as to how to respond. I thought he would begin with a biblical view, but he was more curious to know who the people were that were exhibiting such feelings for another. I played a game of "cat and mouse" bouncing around without answering the question. Then the front door opened and Jonathan came rushing in.

"Sorry Pastor, I had to work late." Your wife and I were just discussing some of the ideas that other members of the church had suggested." Kendrick said. Do you have anything you would like to add to the suggestions?" He asked Jonathan. "No, my wife and I discussed it prior to your arrival so I'm sure she has taken care of everything." Kendrick said his goodbyes and excused himself for the evening. Although Jonathan came home, I knew I succeeded in peaking Kendrick's curiosity.

Kendrick was more curious than expected. The next day after Jonathan left for work Kendrick called. The possibility of who the church members were that was dealing with the issue of having inappropriate feelings had been on his mind. He begged me to tell him the names. I stalled for a very long time before saying, "It is me that is having inappropriate feeling for you." Kendrick grew very silent and couldn't speak a word. He sat there trying to take in the information he had just received. All I could think was that I had made the biggest mistake of my life by telling Kendrick I was having inappropriate feelings toward him.

Finally he spoke, "What made you start having such feelings for me?" he asked. "It just happened one Sunday watching you and then the thoughts wouldn't go away." I responded. He seemed to have been having a hard time believing me at first. Then he asked me what time my husband would be arriving home from work. I told him that I didn't expect him to return until around six that evening. So, Kendrick said that he would be stopping by to discuss the situation in person.

I was nervous and elated at the same time. I didn't know what to expect. Was he going to reject me, was he going to counsel me? Then I thought about Jonathan and whether or not he would find out about my feelings toward Kendrick. If he came over it would be a bad situation, I was a married woman and so was he, I thought.

It wasn't long before Kendrick arrived and rang the doorbell. I knew I was doing something very wrong, but it brought me so much excitement. I answered the door and Kendrick came in. He stood in the foyer staring at me while he contemplated what to do or say next. After refocusing, he told me that he didn't believe what I had said on the phone and he wanted to look me in the eyes to see if this was some type of set up.

As the adrenalin rushed throughout my body I stood on the tip of my toes and kissed him. This was the adrenalin rush of a lifetime I was experiencing. He pulled away in shock as to see if this was really happening. I grabbed his hand and led him to the living room. I gestured for him to take a seat on the sofa. Then I proceeded to get to know him.

It was the most exhilarating thing I had done in my life. I did not know if it was the adrenalin rush or that getting to know Kendrick was as amazing as I dreamed. The thrill of getting caught and knowing that I was doing something forbidden excited me as well. I was beside myself afterwards. I couldn't believe what I had done. Kendrick kissed me good-bye and said he would call me as soon as he got home.

I could not believe it, whoever this woman was, the bad girl in me had been unleashed and I loved her. The wild side of me that had been hidden from the world had finally been set free and I enjoyed all that I had desired.

Kendrick called as soon as he got home as he said. He was still in shock about recent events. Knowing that he was a man of God and having an affair was eating at him inside, but the overwhelming excitement he experienced overtook his rationality of thought. Instead of telling me it would never happen again, we planned our next rendezvous.

Kendrick suggested a place located miles outside of town that few people knew about. With it being so far away he figured we could go without being noticed. I had to put a plan together on how I could get away from my husband, the excuses I could use to leave home. I was anxious to see Kendrick again and nothing was going to stand in my way, not even Jonathan.

The day had finally arrived and I had picked miniature fights with Jonathan all day. I pretended to be so angry that I stormed out. I picked up the car keys and slammed the front door behind me. Jonathan did not understand what was going on. We had always talked out our issues, but this time I was lashing out. Surely, it wasn't that bad, he thought. Jonathan was left there at home with our son confused as to what happened, and I was on my way to meet Kendrick.

I called Kendrick on his cell phone as I had gotten closer to my destination. He gave me directions and as I drove up into the parking lot I noticed him standing at the entrance waiting for me. He was gorgeous standing there. As I took him into my thoughts and all of a sudden I became very nervous. He came out to the car and opened the car door and escorted me inside.

When entering I noticed roses and candles throughout the room. I stood there in amazement. Of all the things I had imagined about Kendrick I did not imagine how romantic he would be. Suddenly, I had butterflies in my stomach and my hands began to sweat. Why was I so nervous? This wasn't our first time together, but this time it was planned.

Kendrick was very kind, we sat on the edge of the bed and we talked for hours. In the midst of our conversation I reached up, touched his face and gently kissed him. Instantly calmness fell over me and I knew Kendrick that night. Kendrick was a gentle man and in everything he did he gave his all. Never at any time was he selfish, but he cared for me. The lust I developed for Kendrick transformed into love that evening, and I never wanted to spend a moment of time away from him.

As the night came to a close I developed a sense of sadness. Kendrick walked me to my car and kissed me goodbye. Tears slowly fell down my cheeks. I didn't understand why I was in tears. Was I sad for what I had done to Jonathan? On my way back home I kept replaying the events of my evening with Kendrick. It was a moment I would never forget. As I got closer to home I dreaded walking through the door and having to face Jonathan.

I knew Jonathan would be upset with me for walking out the house. When I arrived Jonathan was still up waiting for me. "Where have you been?" he said in an angry tone. "I went for a drive and got lost." I said. "Don't you ever walk out on me like that again," He replied. "I was so worried about you." He leaned over to kiss me, but I turned away. Was it that easy to get over on him, I thought.

I went toward our bedroom into the master bathroom and looked myself in the mirror. Perhaps, I should have felt guilty, but when I thought of Kendrick nothing else mattered. I jumped in the shower, changed into my pajamas and went to bed while leaving Jonathan lost in thought, wondering what had gotten into me. I couldn't imagine what would happen if he knew what was going on with Kendrick and I.

My marriage to Jonathan was never the same. I began to see Kendrick more often. He started making up church related excuses so that he and I could be alone with each other. From then on I spent most of my time at the church than I did at home. Kendrick had an outside job that allowed him to take long extended lunches, which he spent with me. Perhaps our spouses were suspicious, but neither one of us cared. We continued on with our affair for months. Being with my husband was almost obsolete. He asked questions, but I evaded them the best I could. Then one day, all of a sudden, Jonathan asked me to have a baby.

I had wanted a child in the past with Jonathan, but he would always tell me it wasn't a good time. Now it wasn't a good time for me. Having a child with Jonathan would mean not being with Kendrick and that was not what I wanted. With all the marital issues we were having, at no fault of Jonathan, he thought that having another child would solve our problems. I knew that the only way to solve our problems would be for me to end the affair with Kendrick. I had to keep Jonathan from being suspicious and so I reluctantly agreed.

Adulterer

The bible defines Adultery not only as a married individual having sexual intercourse with someone that is not his spouse, but also anyone that looks at another with lustful intent has already committed adultery with her in his heart.

> **"You have heard that it was said, 'You shall not commit adultery.' But I say to you that everyone who looks at a woman with lustful intent has already committed adultery with her in his heart.**
>
> **Matthew 5:27-28 (ESV)**

In this passage you learn that Adultery begins with just one thought. It was just one impure thought of Kendrick that led Michelle to Adultery. The dangerous aspects of your thoughts are that it defiles the heart. Remember in chapter one I told you that the enemy had control of the brain function, your thoughts. As Christians we must change how we think.

> **Finally, brothers, whatever is true, whatever is honorable, whatever is just, whatever is pure, whatever is lovely, whatever is commendable, If there is any excellence, if there is anything worthy of praise, think about these things.**
>
> **Philippians 4:8 (ESV)**

Christians, our focus has to be on the things of God. When we think of Godly things it leads to Godly acts, which in turn produces Godliness. If this is true then so is the opposite. When you think ungodly thoughts it produces ungodly acts, which in turn produces ungodliness. Take a moment and think of the production process in your life. Are you producing Godliness or Ungodliness? Just remember that every act first begins with a thought.

To learn the truth of what God has said about the adulterous woman should bring every adulterer falling to their knees with a repentant heart. Proverbs 2:16 states:

> **So you will be delivered from the forbidden woman, from the adulteress with her smooth words, who forsakes the companion of her youth and forgets the covenant of God; for her house sinks down to death, and her paths to the departed; none who go to her come back, nor do they regain the paths of life.**
>
> **Proverbs 2:16-19(ESV)**

This passage of scripture refers to the adulterer as the forbidden woman, meaning she has been banned and you need to keep your distance. God said to stay away from her. Why must we stay away from the adulterous woman? The reason for this as it is said in the scripture her house sinks down to death. She is like quicksand. To the eye she looks stable, but when you take a closer look she is sinking. Her path leads to death.

The adulterer has forgotten the covenant of God. She has broken covenant not only with her husband, but most importantly with God. Christ became our cornerstone, the joining of man to God, and without Him as our Center the relationship becomes undone.

> **Let marriage be held in honor among all, and let the marriage bed be undefiled, for God will judge the sexually immoral and adulterous.**
>
> **Hebrews 13:4(ESV)**

When Michelle married Jonathan she did not honor her marriage. She married ultimately because she did not want to be a single mother. There was nothing honorable about the marriage from the start, but even so she was still married. In turned she defiled the marriage bed, she brought another man into her marriage. Jonathan loved her truly and gave all of himself to her and asked nothing in return.

She dishonored her relationship with God, her husband, Kendrick, Kendrick's wife, and herself. Every act of the adulterous woman is immoral and God will judge.

The book of Ecclesiastes and 1 Corinthians tells us that there is nothing new under the sun. As I researched this topic I found many scenarios describing the adulterous attack that is very similar to Michelle's.

> **There isn't any temptation that you have experienced which is unusual for humans. God, who faithfully keeps his promises, will not allow you to be tempted beyond your power to resist. But when you are tempted, he will also give you the ability to endure the temptation as your way of escape.**
> **1Corinthians 10:13 (GWT)**

God provided Michelle with two obvious ways of escape. He gave her the opportunity to get past the lustfulness in her heart. The first opportunity was when she had her first initial meeting with Kendrick and his wife was present when she arrived. This was an opportunity for her to realize that not only was Kendrick a married man, but she was a married woman and marriage is to be honored.

The second opportunity God gave her was when He took Kendrick out of the country. This was a time to reflect. God gave Michelle the opportunity to get past her lustfulness and focus on her family. She made a conscious decision to give into her temptation. She had the power to resist and the opportunity to walk away, but she chose sin instead.

> **She lies in wait like a robber and increases the traitors among mankind.**
> **Proverbs 23:28 (ESV)**

As you have read, Michelle plotted and planned her seduction on Kendrick. She waited patiently until the right opportunity presented itself for her to let him know just how she was feeling. She lusted after Kendrick and put together a strategic plan to obtain her desired results.

> **The eye of the adulterer also waits for the twilight, saying, 'No eye will see me'; and he veils his face.**
> **Job 24:15 (ESV)**

The adulterer always sneaks and hides in the dark as if no one will catch him/her. When Kendrick and Michelle planned a night together, they planned it during the late night hours in a different town so that no one would be able to see them. One of the first signs in knowing that you shouldn't be doing whatever it is that you are planning is when you have to hide so that no one can see you. God will shine light on darkness so that the truth shall be seen.

> **For the lips of a forbidden *(banned/stay away)* woman drip honey, and her speech is smoother than oil, but in the end she is bitter as wormwood, sharp as a two-edged sword.**
> **Proverbs 5:3-4 (ESV)**

Proverbs 5:3-4 is a very powerful scripture as it relates to the adulterous woman. Let me start out by giving you the definition of bitter. The Advance English Dictionary defines bitter as:

1. Marked by strong resentment or cynicism
2. Very difficult to accept or bear
3. Harsh or corrosive in tone
4. Expressive or sever grief or regret
5. Proceeding from or exhibiting great hostility or animosity
6. Causing a sharp and acrid taste experience
7. Causing a sharply painful or stinging sensation; used especially of cold

After Michelle went through her relationship with Terrance, she developed the listed forms of bitterness. She never thought of herself as being a bitter woman, but after looking up the definition of the word she had to come to grips with who she was during that time. Not only did the scripture tell her that she was bitter, it also referred to her as wormwood.

> **The Third angel blew his trumpet, and a great star fell from Heaven, blazing like a torch, and it fell on a third of the rivers and on the springs of water. The name of the star is Wormwood. A third of the waters became wormwood, and many people died from the water, because it had been made bitter.**
> **Revelation 8:10-11 (ESV)**

Wormwood was poisonous and killed everything it touched or anyone that drank of it. In essence the Bible tells us that the adulterous woman is poisonous, dangerous, and the end result is death. It was hard for Michelle to accept that through her followed death. The bitterness of wormwood is associated with death. A few scriptures below are listed in order to help give you a visual of this fatality.

> **He has filled me with bitterness; he has sated me with wormwood.**
> **Lamentations 3:15 (ESV)**

> **Therefore thus saith the LORD of hosts concerning the prophets; Behold, I will feed them with wormwood, and make them drink the water of gall (*poison*): for from the prophets of Jerusalem is profaneness gone forth into all the land.**
> **Jeremiah 23:15 (KJV)**

> **Therefore thus saith the LORD of hosts, the God of Israel; Behold, I will feed them, even this people, with wormwood, and give them water of gall (*poison*) to drink.**
> **Jeremiah 9:15 (KJV)**

God does not honor nor bless sinful acts. The word of God is clear that the unrighteous will not inherit the kingdom of God.

> **Or do you not know that the unrighteous will not inherit the kingdom of God? Do not be deceived: neither the sexually immoral, nor idolaters, nor adulterers, nor men who practice**

> **homosexuality, nor thieves, nor the greedy, nor drunkards, nor revilers, nor swindlers will inherit the kingdom of God.**
> **1 Corinthians 6:9-10 (ESV)**

Some of you that are reading this book may say that you have never cheated on your husband or wife, but yet you too are still committing adultery. In the book of Jeremiah and Hosea, God speaks of spiritual adultery. You may not have cheated on your spouse, but you have been more committed to your possession, your job, your money, and your family than you have to God. This too is adultery.

> **For you shall not worship no other God, for the Lord, whose name is Jealous, is a jealous God.**
> **Exodus 34:14 (ESV)**

When you place other things before God those thing becomes your God. You have committed adultery. God has and continue to be there for us. He is a God that never change, but we continue to change our minds about Him.

God tells us in Jeremiah chapter two that we used to be devoted and loved like a bride as we followed Him. We have turned from those things and we have become devoted to the things of the world. God repeats our sins in Hosea stating:

> **Hear the word of the Lord, O children of Israel, for the Lord has a controversy with the inhabitants of the land. There is no faithfulness or steadfast love, and no knowledge of God in the land, there is swearing, lying, murder, stealing, and committing adultery. They break all bounds and bloodshed follows bloodshed.**
> **Hosea 4: 1-2 (ESV)**

Adultery, whether physical or spiritual, has major consequences. You can live a life with wilderness experiences out in a desert filled with pits where there are droughts, void, and endless darkness. This is the result of loving the world. With God there are an abundance of blessings, lands of fruits, and only light ahead.

If you want to be blessed, adulterer, I beseech you by the mercies of Jesus Christ to fall on your knees with a heart of repentance and beg for God's forgiveness. There is still hope for the Adulterer and your hope is in Christ Jesus.

Sinfulness

Do you think it's okay to live the life you've been living?
As if you haven't been taught any better.
You're running around the merry-go-round
Doing the same things you've done before.
Have you gotten tired yet from running around in a circle?

My head is spinning watching you loop to loop.
Have you no respect for yourself?
For the temple that God dwells?
If you keep living the way you are living,
Your soul is going straight to hell.

Now you may think I'm judging you,
But I'm just speaking the absolute truth.
I'm only speaking what I already know.
I used to be the star of the show.

You know the old saying "been there; done that"?
Men whispering "here kitty kitty kitty Kat"
At some point you have to get tired of lying on your back.

HIV and AIDS is real you see
And there's no coming back from that disease.
This old world only offers temporary pleasure,
But there's a treasure that lays wait in Heaven.

Throw down those old bags,
And pick up your crown.
You are a child of God!
There is no time for fooling around.

Grace and Mercy have been your close friends,
But sooner rather than later all that's going to end.
Tomorrow is not promised,
So repent without delay,
Turn from your sins and turn to Christ.
Jesus is the only way!

CHAPTER FOUR

Kendrick was not happy about ending the relationship between the two of us. He continued calling me on the phone and coming by the house after Jonathan would leave for work. It was difficult trying to resist his advances toward me. In an effort to make him understand, I explained to him that Jonathan and I were trying to have a baby. Kendrick was stunned at the news, but he didn't see that as a reason to end things between us.

Even in Kendrick's attempts to be respectful he could never let go of the lust that filled him. Kendrick continued to try and see me every opportunity he could. The more he made advances toward me, the weaker I became, but I never gave in. It took a while, but I was finally able to make Kendrick understand that he needed to walk away so I could make things right with Jonathan.

Jonathan and I tried for months to get pregnant. Finally, after four months, I took a home pregnancy test and the results came back positive. Jonathan was happier than ever. Knowing that I was carrying his child meant the world to him. He couldn't wait till the doctor confirmed the pregnancy.

I called the doctor's office to schedule an appointment with the nurse. The nurse told me that I didn't need an appointment, but to just walk into the clinic for a pregnancy test. I skipped all the way to the doctor with excitement. When I arrived at the doctor I was given a lab cup to take home and give a sample first thing the next morning, then bring it back to the lab for testing.

I never made it back to the lab. I went home to rest for the evening, and when I had awaken, I found myself in a pool of blood. I panicked and quickly dialed the on call nurse to find out what I needed to do. She recommended that I lay down with my legs elevated to see if the bleeding would stop. A half hour passed and the bleeding had not stopped. Jonathan picked me up, carried me to the car, and rushed me to the emergency room.

Once I arrived at the emergency room the attendants rushed me to the back. Jonathan stood there in a state of gloominess. He didn't understand what was happening. Finally, a Gynecologist walked in the room and told us the terrible news. "Mr. and Mrs. Smith you miscarried." It was as if darkness fell upon Jonathan.

Jonathan was inconsolable. Having a child was very important to him. His sadness derived both from the loss of the child, but he also believed he was losing me at the same time. This child was his way of making things better in the marriage.

Upon returning home from surgery three days later Jonathan and I finally had the opportunity to console one another. It turned out that the loss of our child brought us closer together. As time went by, I started to see my husband as I did once before, with love and admiration. I saw him for the wonderful man he was. The miscarriage had served a purpose in helping me to see that I did still love Jonathan. At that time I decided to really work on my marriage. Things between us were going great until tragedy struck us again.

Jonathan and I were returning from a day of shopping and as I was climbing the staircase I collapsed. Jonathan panicked and didn't know what to do. Immediately he picked me up and drove me straight to the emergency room. While the emergency staff was wheeling me to a room, I had awoken. Then suddenly a storm of doctors and nurses began asking me questions, while others were probing at my body. After much examination the doctors discovered a ruptured cyst. I was hospitalized for three days after having another surgery. Jonathan stayed by my bedside every day, only to leave at night to rest at home.

While at home on the computer researching my condition he came across my email account, in which I forgot to log out of, and discovered past emails between Kendrick and I detailing our desires and plans for rendezvous. Once he discovered the emails he began searching the home and he came across my personal journal. Jonathan became outraged at what he had found. He did his best to keep his anger buried in order to be there for me while I was in the hospital. After being discharged from the hospital, I returned home with my husband not knowing that my whole world was about to fall apart.

As we arrived home Jonathan carried me to the living room sofa and made sure I was comfortable. He then turned to me and said, "Michelle, we need to talk". He proceeded to ask me if Kendrick was the father of the child we miscarried. I was lost for words. How did he find out about Kendrick? Why was he asking me that question? My mouth opened, but no words came out. After what seemed like a lifetime of stuttering, Jonathan told me that he read my emails and my journal. At this point there was no denying the truth. I had no way to escape. I had no other choice except to confess my sins to him.

I begged Jonathan to forgive me, but at the time he couldn't. He never could have imagined that I would ever do anything to hurt him. I tried to explain to him that he was the father of the baby. My explanations did not console Jonathan, nor did he believe me. In that moment his grieving had come to an end. He realized that he did not know if he was grieving for his child or Kendrick's child. He felt destroyed physically and emotionally. I had just unraveled his entire life. He had every reason not to trust me, but I needed him to trust me now more than ever.

A few days went by and I took it as a good sign that Jonathan had not left home yet. He wasn't speaking to me, but at least he was still there. He came and went through the house, but never spoke a word to me. Any time I tried to be near Jonathan, he would get up and leave the room. I had no idea what was going through his mind, but I knew I needed to give him the time and space to deal with it.

Sunday morning Jonathan arose out of bed earlier than usual. He went to the front of the house, picked up the phone, and called Kendrick. Jonathan face turned red with rage as he said, "Kendrick we need to meet". Kendrick knew immediately that Jonathan found out everything. Nonetheless, Kendrick agreed to meet him.

Jonathan demanded that I get in the car and go with him. I had no idea what was about to happen. I began to fear for my life as well as the life of Kendrick. We drove into an empty parking lot of a grocery store and waited for Kendrick to arrive. Once he arrived, Jonathan stood outside the car door as Kendrick approached him. Kendrick stretched out his arm to shake Jonathan's hand and with hesitation Jonathan walked up to Kendrick, shook his hand, and then they both proceeded to walk around the corner of the building.

My heart started beating at three times its normal rate, and my breathing became heavier and heavier as I imagined the worst. I had no idea what was happening as they both were out of sight. Time began to tick slower as my anticipation grew stronger. Finally, they both emerged into my view of sight and I breathed a sigh of relief.

I had no idea what had been said between Jonathan and Kendrick, but as they approached the car they both had a terrible look on their faces. Jonathan opened my car door and demanded I get out and say goodbye to Kendrick. This was a strange situation, but I decided not to question anything Jonathan said. Kendrick looked me in the eyes and apologized for taking part in the affair. Kendrick told me that Jonathan demanded that he let me go and that I could no longer work at the church anymore. Kendrick gave me a hug and walked away with tears in his eyes. He knew he would never see me again. The ride home with Jonathan was in total silence. I was more afraid of the silence than his anger. I knew I had lost my husband and things would never be the same again.

When we arrived home Jonathan and I went our separate ways. I walked to the bedroom more emotional than I had ever been. I had lost my husband as well as Kendrick. My tears were neither for my husband nor the child we lost, and Jonathan knew it. What was he to do? He loved me more than life itself.

Just as I had known I lost Jonathan, he knew in return that he had lost me. Jonathan worshipped me and even in the midst of an awful situation he wanted nothing more than to make me happy. He could no longer bear seeing me cry tears of loss and so he came to me in a spirit of remorse and said, "Michelle, I love you so much that I would rather see you with Kendrick and happy than to live without you at all." Jonathan told me to get dressed and go to church.

In that moment I understood just how much Jonathan loved me and no matter how much I claimed to have loved him, in that moment I knew I didn't. My desire to see Kendrick outweighed my morality and I got dressed and went to church.

I knew the right thing for me to do was to stay at home and work on my marriage, but the greed and selfishness inside of me wanted to see Kendrick again. I had no respect, love, nor devotion for my husband in that moment as I walked out the door. What was I doing? The affair with Kendrick had already ended. Why was I so torn about not seeing him again?

It didn't register until afterwards that Jonathan was testing me. He was hoping that I loved him enough to walk away from Kendrick and choose him. He was my husband, but I chose my lover, my married lover and it tore Jonathan apart inside.

I arrived at the church and Kendrick was in the middle of teaching a Sunday School lesson. I walked through the door with boldness as if nothing had happened that morning. Kendrick stood as if being in a state of shock. He looked past me to see if Jonathan was going to walk in behind me, but he saw no one. I sat down in the back of the room and waited. Kendrick was unable to continue his lesson due to his astonishment and so he closed out the class early. As everyone left the room, including his wife, we remained behind and talked.

He wanted to know why I was there. I explained to him the conversation Jonathan and I had at home and immediately Kendrick's excitement overtook him and in the middle of the classroom with his wife outside the door, he leaned down and kissed me. We both exited the room with huge smiles on our faces and walked to the sanctuary. I praised the Lord that Sunday, although, the Lord was burning with rage because of my actions. All I knew was that no one would take me away from Kendrick.

In an attempt to go back into hiding I went to Jonathan and apologized for walking out on him. I told him I wanted to work on our marriage and that I would stop seeing Kendrick for good. Jonathan grabbed my hand, kissed me, and forgave me.

I knew I was lying to Jonathan, but I wanted to remain married and be with Kendrick at the same time. I knew I couldn't completely walk away from my marriage while Kendrick was still with his wife.

A month later a conference was taking place out of town. Jonathan was unable to travel with me due to work, so I went alone. Kendrick had paid for my conference registration as well as the hotel room. He was excited about being with me, and so he planned the entire week of things for us to do together while away. Although Kendrick's wife would be accompanying him to the conference he made sure my room would be located where it would be convenient for him to have easy access to me without anyone knowing or seeing.

Kendrick and I made sure not to sign up for any of the same classes as to make sure no one saw us together. On occasion we did have lunch with each other, but no one was the wiser. In the midst of the night Kendrick always made excuses to leave his wife and come down to be with me. One night someone saw him come into my room and became suspicious. Suddenly, there was a knock at the door.

Kendrick had planned out everything and brought along paperwork from the church to place in my room to show that we were discussing church business. I answered the door and one of the brothers asked, "What are you all doing in here?" Kendrick invited him in and showed him what we were working on, or pretending to work on. The brother was none the wiser and shook Pastor's hand and walked away.

The following morning the hotel room phone rang, it was my husband's boss. "Mrs. Smith, I called to let you know that this morning at work your husband collapsed. He has been asking for you." The next thing for me to do should have been simple, but not for me, I was confused. I was torn between going to see about my husband and remaining with Kendrick.

I called up to Kendrick's room and his wife answered the phone. I told her about what happened to Jonathan, and so she and Kendrick both immediately ran down to my room. She offered to drive me back to town to see about him, but Kendrick kept insisting that he would drive me instead. In the midst of the dispute, Jonathan called my room.

I asked what had happened. He said, "I was praying and asked God to take my life if you were still having an affair with Kendrick." I didn't know what to say. In that moment I felt so much guilt, shame, and regret. What could I say? Kendrick and his wife were right there listening to our conversation. I avoided commenting on his statement by telling him I was on my way home to be with him. Jonathan insisted that I stay, once again, and finish out the conference. "I will see you when you get home," he said. I hung up the phone more confused than ever. God did not take his life, but the sign was surely clear.

When I arrived home I told Kendrick that I could not see him again. I was truly ending the affair. I was finally ready to make my marriage work truly and honestly, but I knew in order for that to work Kendrick had to be out of the picture completely. Jonathan was still having a difficult time dealing with the affair. For weeks my husband and I walked around the house as total strangers. In an effort to rekindle our marriage, Jonathan had arranged a family vacation to New York. This would be the vacation we needed. This will be the trip to bring our marriage back into perspective for us both.

When we arrived in New York I was so excited, but Jonathan seemed to be in another world. He spent a lot of time by himself. One night as we were getting ready for bed, I sat on the edge of the bed, trying not to invade his space, and looked him in the eyes and told him that I did not want a divorce. He hesitated and told me that he did not want a divorce either, but it was an issue that would take him a while to get over, if at all. He tried to make an effort and leaned over and kissed me on the cheek. That kiss was the only touch I had received from Jonathan since finding out about the affair. From that day forward, while on vacation, Jonathan and I seemed closer than ever before and thoughts of Kendrick was far from my mind.

We returned home with plans of making a new start. Jonathan forgave me, but I knew I had to work extremely hard at earning back his trust back. I had been a fool to cheat on my husband. I couldn't change the past, but I was sure going to change the future.

While having dinner one night the phone rang. Jonathan answered, but he did not speak. I thought it was strange, but I didn't say anything. After a few seconds he hung up the phone. Then curiosity got the best of me. "Who was that on the phone sweet heart?" I asked. Jonathan paused for a moment before leaving the table, without speaking a word to me, and walked out the front door. I knew then that Kendrick had called and Jonathan assumed we were still together.

I sat at the table with my son as he finished his dinner. I was panicking on the inside. Where had Jonathan gone? Why? Is he coming back? I became so worried. After a few hours had passed, Jonathan came home, but he was not alone. Jonathan feared that he would not be able to control his temper, therefore he asked his supervisor at work to accompany him home. Just as quietly as Jonathan left the dinner table, he packed a bag and walked out the house. Right as he was closing the door Jonathan said, "I want a divorce."

I was a horrible wife and mother. Who could blame Jonathan? He probably stayed longer than any man would have, but at the same time it was hard to understand why this was happening. I had finally ended the affair and was trying to give my marriage a real chance, but I had waited too late.

Darkness

Darkness is defined as wickedness or evil; having the absence of light. In churches across the nation there are people that have come in among the Body of Christ portraying a falsified persona of Christianity. They look the part and act the part in public, but in the night behind closed doors, there lies wickedness (darkness).

> **But if anyone walks in the night, he stumbles, because the light is not in him.**
> **John 11:10 (ESV)**

Michelle portrayed herself as a Christian, but she lived a life of darkness. She confessed Christianity, but her life was contradictory to that fact. Michelle lived in darkness until darkness overtook her. At the same time the enemy would still tell her there was nothing wrong with what she was doing and that she could still be a Christian while all along committing adultery.

Too often as Christians we do not want to admit nor accept we are in darkness. We continue to call ourselves Christians while at the same time we are living a sinful life. The enemy is out seeking to destroy the church, and living a falsified life gives satan all the ammunition he needs.

> **The thief cometh not, but for to steal, and to kill, and to destroy: I am come that they might have life, and that they might have it more abundantly.**
> **John 10:10 (KJV)**

Man does not separate the sinner from the Church. It is not the sinner that is a hypocrite, liar, thief, adulterer or idolater, it is the Church. The actions of one sinner has a greater impact on those around them (the church) than themselves.

> **If we say we have fellowship with him while we walk in darkness, we lie and do not practice the truth.**
>
> **1 John 1: 6 (ESV)**

Michelle lived a life of a liar, she confessed Christianity, but she walked in darkness. God had given her several opportunities to repent and return to Him, not just him, but to her husband as well. Michelle was so far in her sin that it consumed her to the point of having no regard toward man's feelings.

I would like to take the time to define the word Christian. Many people have different meaning of what they believe Christian to mean. They often take bible doctrine out of context in order to mold the definition to shape who they are. In the end there is no falsifying the definition. Let us take the time to break the word down so that it makes sense. The first word you see when looking at Christ-ian is Christ. Christ is our Lord and savior whom lived a blameless life and walked in obedience to God until death. He knew no sin, but bore our sins upon the cross. The suffix –ian means relating to, belonging to, and resembling. Now we cannot eliminate part of the definition of –ian. The definition is all inclusive. We are related to Christ because we have been adopted into the family of God.

> **He predestined us for adoption as sons through Jesus Christ, according to the purpose of His**

will, to the praise of his glorious grace, with
which he has blessed us in the Beloved.

Ephesians 1:5-6 (ESV)

Not only have we been adopted into the family, we now belong to Him. God is the father, our headship that created all things for His purpose and glory. This leads us to resembling Christ. We must look like him. Who we are must be the very essence of who Christ is. God has called us to be Holy and blameless. Christ lived a life of perfection, without sin. Not that we will reach perfection in this life, but we shall be striving for perfection at all times, to be like Christ.

Christians, there is a way out of sin. The first step toward Christ is to confess our sins. We must admit and accept where we are. If you are living a life of denial, thinking you are okay, you are doing more harm than good. You are inevitably sinking further into the black hole that is your life. You're broken and you need God's redeeming love and mercy to snatch you, with force, immediately from darkness.

Therefore, confess your sins to one another and
pray for one another, that you may be healed
(restored). The prayer of a righteous person has
great power as it is working.

James 5:16 (ESV)

Go before God repenting of your sins, and asking Him to restore you. God is the God of restoration.

And after you have suffered a little while, the
God of all grace, who has called you to his
eternal glory in Christ, will himself restore,
confirm, strengthen, and establish you.

1 Peter 5:10 (ESV)

**Behold, I will bring to it health and healing, and
I will heal them and reveal to them abundance
of prosperity and security. I will restore the
fortunes of Judah and the fortunes of Israel,
and rebuild them as they were at first.**
Jeremiah 33:6-7 (ESV)

Who you were is not who you are now. Your past does not define you, but it creates a better you in Christ Jesus. God has saved and redeemed you and you are no longer in darkness, but you can now ravish in God's glorious light.

Me

What is this strange thing that lives inside of me?
Seeing parts of me I don't even see.
What are you?
You Stranger, You Murderer, You thief!
Come out! Come out! Come out of me!
You destroy the very essence of my being.
I didn't invite you in to take over me.
You are a thief! That's who you are.
You stole that which was most valued to me.
Something I can never get back.
Now that you have touched it,
It's not worth what is used to be.
It has depreciated in value,
And now men think it's free.
You are a murder! Yes that is who you are.
You killed the good that once was a part of me.
Now my thoughts have changed,
And not for the better.
You saw that I was vulnerable, weak and naive.
You crept in like a thief to destroy me.
You took what was good, and then put me to sleep.
When I awaken,
I was not the same.
I now had to live with the guilt and the shame.
Everywhere I turn people see who I really am.
The sin I wear is dark,
With such an awful smell.
Everything I touch I destroy.
Some of your character traits I deploy.
My head hangs down in shame,

For the hypocrite that I am.
Trying to tell someone how to live their life,
When I cannot do the same.
I am living a lie.
Don't believe a word I say,
For it comes from a dark place.
Live and let live they say,
But I pray that God will let a dirty rag
like me see another day!

CHAPTER FIVE

It was days before I heard from Jonathan again. I tried calling him, but he wouldn't answer his phone. I left messages begging him to forgive me and come home. I knew there was nothing I could do and that I had lost him. Jonathan had always given me what I wanted. He could never say no to me, but now things had changed, and the hold I once had on him was no more. I spent my days without Jonathan locked in the house shattered and trying to hold it together for my son, but it had been the most difficult thing to do.

I had neglected my son throughout the entire affair, leaving him and Jonathan alone on many nights. I had not been a good parent and I definitely didn't know how to be one without Jonathan. I had married Jonathan so that I would have a partner in raising my son, but now all of that was coming to an end.

A couple of weeks had gone by and Jonathan came over unexpectedly to check on our son and me. Despite the pain I caused him I knew he still cared. I knew I had to act quickly if I was going to win him back. This visit was going to be my opportunity to change his mind about divorce. After playing with our son for the evening, Jonathan laid him down to sleep. He decided not to leave immediately, but wanted to sit and talk. I knew he was not going to listen to anything I had to say, so I waited for him to speak. As I waited, Jonathan never said a word. "I miss you," I blurted out. I then leaned over toward Johnathan in an attempt to let him know I desired him. To my surprise Jonathan reciprocated the same desires.

The evening came to an end and I had no desire for Jonathan to leave. I pleaded with him to stay, but when he refused I knew he had not gotten over what happened between Kendrick and me. I saw my world collapsing to its death. I knew I had ruined my marriage, but I wanted to work things out now more than ever.

I couldn't imagine life without Jonathan. As Jonathan headed toward the front door, I rushed to the kitchen, grabbed the sharpest knife in the room and slid the blade across my wrist. As the blood gushed from my arm, I thought to myself, this was the final end to the destruction I had caused. I had wanted both worlds, but the illusion of me having both worlds never coincided with reality.

Jonathan ran to me and tried to stop the bleeding while at the same time dialing the police. He was terrified of what I had done. I looked up at him and saw tears flowing from his eyes. "Why couldn't I love this man before?" I thought to myself as I watched him try to save me. He loved me with all that he had and it wasn't enough for me, and yet I was still hurting him by doing this selfish and cowardly thing to escape all the hurt I had caused.

The ambulance arrived and stopped the bleeding. In the midst of the EMT assisting me, Jonathan tried to breathe a sigh of release. The EMT tried taking me to the hospital, but I refused. I demanded Jonathan take me to the master bedroom so that I may rest. I promised him that I would be okay and wouldn't try hurting myself again. Based on that promise to him, he carried me to my room and sat with me until I fell asleep.

Although, Jonathan cared for me he knew now more than ever that he had to leave me. He couldn't bare me continuously putting him through anguish. He kissed me on my forehead as I slept and he left. When I awakened the next morning I was disappointed not to see him there. I checked the house and he was nowhere to be found.

I knew I had to move on and focus on getting myself together. The first start to getting better was fixing me a hot breakfast. I walked into the kitchen to cook some eggs, and as I opened the utensil drawer I noticed that only spoons were there. I began to look throughout the kitchen and saw that everything had been taken. I realized that Jonathan had taken all the knives, forks, and scissors. Anything he thought I could use to hurt myself again. I knew he couldn't be with me, but I also knew he still cared.

Now Kendrick soon found out that Jonathan had moved out, which prompted him to try and reconnect with me. I was trying to deal with the fact that I had lost Jonathan and for Kendrick to be around would make that more difficult to do.

I had officially left the church and had no intentions of returning. I tried all I could to avoid any contact with Kendrick, but he was very persistent. I figured after a while he would give up, but he never did. Everywhere I turned Kendrick was there. I wanted him out of my life for good and nothing I tried worked.

A few weeks went by and Kendrick's wife Tracy and Sister Lauren from the church reached out to me to inquire why I had left the church. They went to Kendrick first, but he did not offer any explanation, which made them even more curious. I attempted to avoid them, but they proved to be more determined than I thought.

On Wednesday evening the doorbell rang and on the other side of the door there stood Tracy and Sister Lauren. I knew I couldn't avoid them any longer. I answered the door and offered them a seat at the dining room table. They both noticed I had been crying, "Michelle, how have you been," Sister Lauren asked. "I can't lie and say I'm okay, but what I will say is that I will be okay," I replied.

They began to discuss with me the lesson that had just concluded at Bible Study, but I had no desire to listen. They tried to ignore the fact that I was zoning them out, but had hopes that something that was being said would provoke a reaction from me. Tracy turned and asked, "What's wrong?" I wanted so much to scream out and let Tracy know that I had been having an affair with her husband, but I couldn't imagine what she would do if I had told her the truth. Tracy and Sister Lauren realized that I wasn't going to share the truth with them and so they asked to pray with me before leaving.

Sister Lauren was not content with leaving my house without answers, therefore she returned the next day alone. I knew she wasn't going to accept my silence. We sat at the dining room table and as she sincerely looked at me, I began to cry. "What's wrong, Sister Smith?" she said. Through the tears I told her that Jonathan had left me after finding out that I was having an affair with the Pastor. "The Pastor!" Sister Lauren responded. "Yes, Kendrick and I have been having an affair for the past year".

Sister Lauren couldn't believe what she was hearing. She was none responsive for what seemed like an eternity. I couldn't believe that the truth was finally out, but I knew it wasn't the end. There was more trouble and distress to come now that Sister Lauren knew.

Sister Lauren comforted me and told me that it wasn't my fault, and the fact that Kendrick was the Pastor, he should have known better. "It's not your fault." She continued repeating to me. After hearing her voice in my ear, repeating the same message, I began to look at myself as a victim. Sister Lauren took my hand and told me she had to leave, but would return.

A few hours later the phone rang, it was Kendrick. Kendrick was furious with me. It turned out that when Sister Lauren left my house she went home and told her husband the events of what had happened. They both had agreed to go and speak with Kendrick and force him to confess to his wife.

Kendrick lived by a cheaters creed, no matter what happens you never admit the truth-LIE-LIE-LIE, even if the proof is put before you. At this point Kendrick had no choice and before he could tell his wife the truth he needed to know why I had betrayed him.

Around one o'clock that morning Kendrick called and asked me to meet him a few blocks away. It was just my son and I now, and there was no one to leave him home with in order for me to meet Kendrick. "What's going on Kendrick?" I asked. He explained that Tracy knew everything and that she was taking things very hard. Kendrick continued to tell me that while he was laying on the sofa sleeping that evening, due to Tracy kicking him out of the bedroom, she came in with a knife and tried to stab him. He had gotten the knife away from her, but had to leave the house immediately.

Kendrick and I had made a mess of things and neither of us knew how to fix it. We sat for hours on the phone talking about what a mess we had made and all the choices we could have made. What were we both to do? Two marriages had fallen apart and not only did we hurt our spouses, the children were hurt, and the church as well. The only thing we both knew was that there was no more hiding.

I had no idea how much damage an affair between Kendrick and I would cause. This affair not only caused division in our church, it affected other churches in the area. People were in a mass panic. The church members didn't understand how their Pastor could allow something like this to happen. It wasn't just Kendrick that was made to look bad, but members throughout the community questioned the commitment of their own Pastors. The church community was in devastation, and it was all because of me. I willingly allowed the spirit of lust to consume me. I had started it all and now I had to live with the fact that my actions had caused many to turn away from Christ.

The humiliation was too much for Jonathan to bear. He felt ashamed and blamed himself for allowing himself to love me, only to be hurt the way he had been. If only he had listened to his parents when they told him to call off the engagement. Jonathan began making travel arrangements for me to return to Tennessee. He felt that if he got rid of me he could begin to heal.

My life had been ruined at my own hands and all I could think about was that I had no job, no money, and the one thing I tried avoiding ultimately came to pass, I was a single mother. After a while my sadness turned into anger and I took my anger out on everyone that was in my line of sight. I suddenly refused to go back, only to have to face another humiliation.

I developed a plan to get rid of the airline tickets. I wouldn't be able to leave without those tickets. Jonathan wouldn't be able to get rid of me just yet. The time it would take him to purchase new tickets would allow me enough time to figure things out.

I knew that if I hid the tickets around the house Jonathan would find them, so I burned them in the Kitchen sink. A few days later Jonathan had contacted me to inform me that the movers were coming to pack up the house. I told him that I didn't see why he was sending the movers as I had no intentions of leaving. I inform him that I no longer had the tickets.

Once again I had made Jonathan furious. It was less than thirty minutes before Jonathan and his boss were knocking on the door. He stormed through the house tearing it apart looking for those tickets. I knew he wasn't going to find them, so I just sat calmly on the sofa flipping through the television channels. After he realized they weren't there he barged into the living room where I was sitting and almost strangled me.

Jonathan had previously been a black belt prior to us marrying. He used his training to control his anger, but I had pushed him to his limit. Jonathan had to cancel all flight plans and made arrangements to get replacement tickets for me to travel. While Jonathan was busy making his arrangements, I had finalized everything I needed to do to ensure that everything back home was in order.

While Kendrick's wife was dealing with having an unfaithful husband she spent a lot of time working and traveling. Her being away and not at home working on the marriage opened the gate for Kendrick and me to rekindle our relationship. The damage had been done and divorce was inevitable, therefore neither of us had a reason to be alone, and so we turned to one another.

The decision for us to continue seeing one another was not as private as it had been in the past. Although, we were not in public prancing our relationship, our friends and family members knew that Kendrick and I were together. This time around, Kendrick and I were able to finally date one another, something we couldn't do in hiding.

Sin Exposed

Expose: make known to the public that was previously known only to a few people or that was meant to be kept secret. (Advance English Dictionary)

But all things that reproved are made manifest by the light; for whatsoever doth make manifest is light.
Ephesians 5:13 (KJV)

There are many who confess Christ, but live in darkness. This will serve as a warning to let you know that God will expose your sin publically. Christians have lived in the world and adapted to its sinful nature, but if the Holy Spirit dwells in you it will convict you, confirming that God has not removed His hand from you. If you continue in your sinful state God will shine light on you and expose you for the sinner you are.

There were opportunities where God had given Michelle warnings about her sinful nature. He exposed her only to her husband and he forgave her. In Michelle's husband's forgiveness, God had shown her mercy. She didn't deserve his forgiveness, but because he loved her, he forgave. This was the perfect opportunity for Michelle to repent and turn from her sin, but instead she ran toward sin harder and faster than before.

Sin can only hide in darkness when there is no light to expose it. God is light and He will not allow you to diminish His name as you confess Christianity before man and live in such a sinful way behind closed doors.

Do not be deceived: God is not mocked, for whatever one sows that will he also reap.
Galatians 6:7 (ESV)

In the book of Jeremiah, God had given Judah numerous opportunities to turn from their sin and repent. Judah continued on and paying no attention to the many warnings of God. God laid out the plan for Judah right before them. God told Judah that He was going to expose them and humiliate them in front of all their enemies. God has to use drastic measures sometimes to bring his people down to their knees in a spirit of repentance.

Growing up Michelle had always heard Galatians 6:7, but it wasn't until she had gone deeper into her sin when she began to really think about it. She knew God was not pleased with her behavior and that she had to suffer in the judgment of what was to come.

When you're so deep in sin and the judgment of God does not strike fear or reverence in you, you're at the point where your sin has consumed you.

Therefore do not pronounce judgment before the time, before the Lord comes, who will bring to light the things now hidden in darkness and will disclose the purposes of the heart. Then each one will receive his commendation from God.
1 Corinthians 4:5 (ESV)

Michelle confessed Christ and lived in darkness to hide her sins from the Church. Darkness had a strong hold on her. She was unable to escape it. God exposed her motives to Jonathan. He had finally realized the true purpose of Michelle marrying him. God exposed her as a betrayer to Tracy. Michelle went into Tracy's home, ate at her table and then slept with her husband. God exposed Michelle as a sinner before the Church. She worshipped in Sunday School, Bible Study, and Sunday morning Worship Service and she lived in darkness.

The entire time her sin was hidden right under their noses and no one knew what was happening. Michelle believed she was untouchable and unseen through it all. Until God shed light on her situation to let her know that He sees all things.

> **The eyes of the Lord are in every place, keeping watch on the evil and the good.**
> **Proverbs 15:3 (ESV)**

Although, man did not see her for the true evil that dwelled in her, God did. He watched and waited the entire year. He knew just the day and hour to expose her. He allowed her to sin over and over and over again while sharing His mercy with her. God showed Michelle mercy as she continued to turn her back on Him. Michelle loved the darkness that dwelled in her and refused to let it go. Sure, there were times when she thought about repenting. She actually tried a few times, but whenever sin knocked at her door she was obliged to answer it.

God loves you and because of that love, He will expose you. God does not expose you in order to laugh in your face. He exposes you so that you can come out of hiding and run to His throne of Grace and ask for forgiveness.

> **But your iniquities have made a separation between you and your God; and your sins have hidden His face from you, so that He does not hear.**
> **Isaiah 59:2 (ESV)**

Michelle was lost. Sin had promised her happiness and pleasure. Sin promised that nothing bad would happen. Sin promised no one would find out. Sin promised that she could live in both worlds and still be a Christian. Sin lied and she never received any of its promises. Believing in the promises of sin led her to hopelessness and despair. She lost everything that she loved and saw no way out except through death. For Michelle to take my own life seemed to be a much better solution than having to be exposed for the sinner she was. She knew she was a coward, an unbeliever of the Word of God.

No matter what you have done, remember that there is a way out. There is hope for you and that hope is in Christ Jesus. God is ready and waiting to forgive and restore you. If you are in sin run now, without delay, and repent of your sin. Whatever sin has promised you know that it will not come to pass, but the promise of God is a guarantee and leads to eternal life.

Warfare

Speak to me, O'God,
let me hear your voice.
The enemy has come to destroy.
I'm caught in this battle
That looks like I'm losing.

I was strong-I was courageous,
I stood in the midst of a war just like David.
Only I wasn't fighting Goliath,
it was a war against myself.

I knew right from wrong,
but I grew weary of well doing.
Disobedience causes dismay,
leaving an open womb of the Spirit
that only God can convey.

Lord, I'm crying out to you,
please don't leave me alone.
Night after night I toss and turn
in fear that the battle could not be won.

Lord, Lord, take over me,
for this is an enemy only you can defeat.
In me I am weak,
but in Thee I am strong.
For the battle I tried to fight
was a battle not of my own.

CHAPTER SIX

A few days prior to my flight leaving, Kendrick came to me and told me that his wife had decided to forgive him. She told him that 14 years of marriage and two children were too much to throw away. "It doesn't matter, Kendrick," I said to him. "You and I have a future together now and you can still be a father to your children. I would not take that away from you." Kendrick couldn't imagine being apart from his children. His father had left him and his mother, and he refused to do the same thing to his children. I was distraught. My whole world had come crashing down once again.

At this point I had lost everything. I had lost my husband and I lost Kendrick. It was difficult dealing with what was happening, but I still had my son, although I didn't deserve him. I couldn't wait to leave California now and make a new start. A few days later I was on a flight to Tennessee filled with despair and determined not to look back. It was finished and there was nothing I could do, but start over.

I arrived in Tennessee and realized I had to face everyone I knew. I had to live with the guilt and shame of a failed marriage and single parenthood. I didn't know how to face my family nor the public. My mother had made it very clear of her disappointment in me. She had high hopes and was happy

I was living a successful life. Now all her hopes for me where no greater than the hope of those that came before me.

I had to face the fact that I brought my suffering upon myself. I couldn't really believe that Jonathan continued as long as he did. He loved me and I took advantage of his love. I deserved to suffer in the consequences of my actions. It wasn't Jonathan that left me, it was I who had left him. I had allowed the lust of another man to tear my marriage apart and now my son had to live without a father.

I had been home only a few days before Kendrick started calling me. He claimed to have missed me and didn't want me to give up on him. I was confused by his words. Why should I linger in hopes of him being with me? His wife had forgiven him and he agreed to stay. Was I supposed to hang around hoping for something that was never going to happen?

Kendrick had gotten my hopes up once and disappointed me, but I couldn't allow it to happen again. As soon as my guard was put up it came crumbling down after Kendrick told me that he wanted to have a child with me. If Kendrick and I had a child together that meant that we would always be together. Had he changed his mind about staying with his wife?

Kendrick and I spoke on the phone often, three or four times a day. I was getting excited. Kendrick was preparing for a trip that would allow him to come stay with me for a few days. We were going to take the opportunity to work toward having a child together. I was so excited.

When Tracy first forgave Kendrick they had decided to try and have another child together too, in an attempt to save the marriage. After their last child Kendrick had a vasectomy, but since his wife was asking for another baby it was the perfect opportunity to have the surgery without any suspicions. His vasectomy reversal was not to get Tracy pregnant, but so that we could have a child of our own.

Kendrick had finally arrived in Tennessee and it was like we had never been apart. I asked my mother to watch after my son as I spent a week away with Kendrick. He had taken me out for candle light dinners, movies, and walks around town. It was so romantic. This is the way things should have always been, I thought.

I was not thrilled when Kendrick had to leave. I never wanted us to separate again. As he departed it felt as if I was losing him all over again. I tried to hold on to the hope that I was possibly carrying his child. This way Kendrick would always be with me.

After Kendrick arrived back home we didn't speak on the phone as often as before. He was always sneaking to talk to me and was never answering his phone. I didn't understand why. He was preparing to leave Tracy so that we could be together, but why was he avoiding me?

It was okay, I told myself quite often. I thought, Once I find out that I'm pregnant things would go back to normal. After a couple of weeks I took a pregnancy test and the results were negative. I called Kendrick and told him the bad news, but he seemed to have already known.

Kendrick had lied to me about having his vasectomy reversed. He tried making excuses for why he didn't have the surgery, but I didn't care. There was no excuse for him making me believe that we were having a child together. This wasn't the beginning of his lies. He had lied to me about everything. He had no intentions of filing for divorce. Although, he was still cheating on Tracy, his marriage meant more to him than I ever did. It was an affair for him and I was the one being torn apart from it.

I grew very frustrated and tired of Kendrick's games. I had been his fool for far too long without any benefits in the end. I had lost everything, I refused to continue in my foolishness. I told Kendrick that the affair was over and I didn't want to hear from him ever again. I knew Kendrick wasn't going to listen. He loved living in both worlds just as much as I did. In order to accomplish this I knew I had to take further measures. The next day I went and changed all my phone numbers.

It had been a while since I had been to church. After everything that happened all I could think about was my relationship with God. It was nonexistent, but I needed Him more than ever in order to get through my ordeal. I spent the next few days in prayer asking God to forgive and restore me, but the guilt of what I had done was eating me alive. I didn't deserve God's forgiveness nor did I believe He would give it to me. I had done horrible things and now reality was setting in.

When Sunday had come around I went back to my home Church where I had grew up. No one in Lexington knew why my marriage had ended, except family. So, going back to church didn't seem to be so embarrassing. If anyone asked about Jonathan, I was going to lie. I knew it was wrong, but I didn't want anyone passing judgment on me. Thankfully, the Church was just happy to have me back home. No one mentioned a word about Jonathan and I was thrilled.

After being back in the Church for a few months I became heavily involved in Church Ministry and devoted myself back to God. I was still working on forgiving myself of my indiscretions, but I was on the right track. I was finally getting myself together. During this time I had found employment and moved out of my mother's house.

Kendrick kept trying to get in touch with me, and then one day he was finally successful. He had called my mother and begged her so many times for my new phone number until she grew tired and gave it to him. He then began calling me nonstop once again. Kendrick had become so obsessed with trying to get in touch with me that Tracy couldn't take it anymore. Once he did reach me he informed me that Tracy had left him and took the children with her.

I knew I couldn't fall back into my old patterns and I dismissed Kendrick statements. I was not going to fall for his lies again. I continued to insist that he stop calling, but for months the calls continued to come. I was over him and he needed to understand that our past would be no more. In the midst of it all Kendrick did not stop trying. He became so obsessed that he flew to Lexington to see me once again. I had developed strong will power over the phone, but face to face would be another story.

When Kendrick arrived I was as prepared as I could be. I had prayed and motivated myself, and planned my rebuttals for whatever it was he had to say. I had been defenseless when it came to Kendrick in the past, but I was stronger and determined now more than ever.

Kendrick was surprised that his visit was not as he had planned. I was weak when it came to Kendrick, and he knew it. He planned to prey on that weakness as his way back into my life, but I had changed. I was different. I was not the same woman he met a year ago. He couldn't believe it. He was in such disbelief and disappointment as I sent him away.

God's forgiveness

Forgiveness is defined as God's restoration of relationship that entails the removal of objective guilt. One of the hardest things for Michelle to do was to ask God to forgive her as well as forgiving herself. She had betrayed her husband, neglected her son, and caused division in the Church. Michelle thought it was the worst thing a person could have done. "Why would God even want for forgiver her?" She thought.

For the wages of sin is death, but the free gift of God is eternal life in Christ Jesus our Lord.
Romans 6:23 (ESV)

God has given us eternal life and it didn't cost us anything. The only person that paid the price was Christ. Christ said I am going to die for you, and through my death I'm granting you life. Who would do such a thing, except a great God? Through Christ's death we are given life, but through sin life is taken from us.

Instead of receiving such a great gift, Michelle inevitable told God she didn't want it.

How much more will the blood of Christ, who through the eternal Spirit offered himself without blemish to God, purify our conscience from dead works to serve the living God.
Hebrew 9:14 (ESV)

Michelle knew that adultery was wrong, but she loved sinning. At the time she felt it was liberating to not have to be the "good girl". We are not taught how to sin we are born sinners through the fall of Adam and Eve.

> But we are all as an unclean thing, and all our
> righteousness are as filthy rags; and we all do
> fade as a leaf; and our iniquities, like the wind,
> have taken us away.
>
> Isaiah 64:6 (KJV)

Obedience is a learned character and Michelle's mother taught her well, but she still rebelled. She wanted to do what she desired and not what God required. Our righteousness, how we justify our morality is described in Isaiah as a filthy rag. Just think about how you would feel if you went to visit a friend, and they had filthy rags laying around the house. Filthy rags create an awful stench and this is what sin does. Sin has a stench about it that the righteousness of God can't bear to be around. Inevitable the separation between you and God manifest death. A life without God is no life at all.

Sometimes we think of being obedient as a restriction, as if it bounds us up. We don't realize that it's just the opposite. There is so much freedom in obedience, but in sin you are restricted and there is nowhere to go, but down. When you're living in God's magnificent light there is no limit to your liberties in Christ. You have the opportunity to be in dark places and shine light upon it.

The reason God allows our sins to be exposed, as I stated in the previous chapter, is to lead us to repentance. A repentant spirit leads you from darkness to light. What many don't understand is that repentance is not just mere words being spoken, it requires action behind it. This is why man cannot repent out of self. He needs God, the Holy Spirit, to lead him to true repentance.

> Therefore, O King Agrippa, I was not disobedient
> to the heavenly vision, but declared first to

> those in Damascus, then in Jerusalem and
> throughout all the region of Judea, and also to
> the Gentiles, that they should repent and turn
> to God, performing deeds in keeping with their
> repentance.
>
> Acts 26:20 (ESV)

The Apostle Paul tells us that after we repent our deeds, what we do next, should be to walk in obedience. When we ask God to forgive us, but continue to live in such a manner that displeases God is not repentance at all. Plainly put, it's just a bunch of words that mean absolutely nothing. Repentance brings about a change in your behavior. God is more than willing to forgive you. God not only forgives, but he forgets. He says, it's done and over with, and I don't want to think about it anymore.

> And no longer shall each one teach his neighbor
> and each his brother, saying, "Know the Lord,"
> for they shall all know me, from the least of
> them to the greatest, declares the Lord. For I
> will forgive their iniquities, and I will remember
> their sin no more.
>
> Jeremiah 31:34 (ESV)

The reason Michelle had such a hard time forgiving herself is because she would not allow herself to forget what she had done. Michelle harbored all the guilt and shame of her actions and would not allow herself to move on. In order for her to accept God's forgiveness, she had to learn to forgive herself.

Michelle had to realize that holding on to her sin was a trick from the enemy. As long as she held on to it, the easier it was for the enemy to suck her back into sin. The enemy wants to keep you in bondage and held up from receiving life from Christ. Satan promotes death, Satan is death and the stench of death is pleasing to the enemy.

God has a sweetness about His forgiveness. His forgiveness is merciful. When God forgives you, He is accepting you back into the family. You're not put on display or made a mockery of. He restores you completely as if nothing happened. I am in no way saying that you will not be disciplined for your rebellion, but even in His disciplined there is sweetness.

> **Bless the Lord, O my soul, and forget not all his benefits, who forgives all your iniquity, who heals all your diseases, who redeems your life from the pit, who crowns you with steadfast love and mercy, who satisfies you with good so that your youth is renewed like the eagles. The Lord works righteousness and justice for all who are oppressed. He made known his ways to Moses, his acts to the people of Israel. The Lord is merciful and gracious, slow to anger and abounding in steadfast love. He will not always chide, nor will he keep his anger forever. He does no deal with us according to our sins, nor repay us according to our iniquities.**
> **Psalms 103:2-10 (ESV)**

Now who can imagine forgiveness being as amazing as David described it in Psalms 103? David knew firsthand what it was like to receive God's forgiveness, and not the punishment he deserved. Just as God forgave David and the many that came after him, God forgave Michelle and after much work she forgave herself.

Nicole Miles

If you are in need of God's forgiveness, He is ready and willing to do so. Go to God in sincerity and ask Him to forgive you. God loves you!

Restoration

How sweet is your grace?
How precious is your mercy?
Day by day you keep me from suffering
you love me in spite of,
and bless me out of love.
I'll open my eyes toward Heaven above.

I rebelled against your word,
and surrounded myself with darkness.
I liked what I loved,
and embraced the hell that is this world.

You had a plan for me,
although I did not know.
Even the evil I did was part of your purpose.

This does not excuse your love I abused,
but it gives me hope for our relationship to be restored.
Forgive me God of the evil I've done,
I'm sorry for neglecting your name.

You are Holy,
you are Righteous,
you were there in the beginning,
to you there is no end.
Your son you gave to me
that my life it would be saved.
Strengthen me God to live in your way.

Here I am,
take all of me,
as I reverence your name.
You are Lord and I am me,
as I take my seat
and bow at your feet.

CHAPTER SEVEN

I had settled into my life in Lexington. My life was finally on track without having the shadow of Kendrick following me around. Things were looking up. I was back in Church, I had the perfect apartment, and a comfortable job I loved. I enrolled in school, and finally started being the mother that my son needed.

I really enjoyed the ministries I was involved in at Church. I was the youngest member on the Usher Board. Anytime there was an event, I was there. Not because I had to be, but because I loved being in the house of God. God was finally pleased with my life. I was intrigued to learn all I could about God and this was the perfect place to do so.

One week as Sunday School was closing out I overheard a couple of older women discussing a married couple. I didn't know who they were talking about, but I overhead them say that the wife needed to hurry back home, before someone else catches his eye. I paid it no attention. I thought it was just a bunch of old women gossiping about things that didn't concern them, soon and very soon I was to find out exactly who the conversation was about.

One Saturday afternoon, as I was playing soccer in the front yard with my son, a black sedan pulled up and the voice of Reverend James Washington called out to me. "I didn't know you lived here," he said. I was stunned to see him, but I was polite and walked over to greet him. "I live across the street in the blue house." He said. I really didn't know what to say because I had never spoken to him before, but I tried being polite. I began to feel a bit awkward, and so I told him I had to go inside and prepare dinner for my son.

The next Sunday at Church James made it a point to stop and speak to me. He tried carrying conversation, but I was busy and so I brushed him off. Again I heard the same old ladies discussing the same marriage, but this time I knew exactly who they were talking about.

One Friday night I was sitting in my living room watching a movie, and there was a knock at the door, it was James. I opened the door and he immediately asked if he could come in. Although I was uncomfortable with him being in my apartment, I allowed him to come in, against my better Judgement. I sat him in the front window at a table with all the lights on in the apartment, so there was a view from the street.

James inquired about why I returned to Tennessee. I told him little as possible. I didn't want my past being gossiped about all over the Church. I explained that my husband was away on business and since he traveled a lot I returned home to be close to my family.

Once he saw that I wasn't divulging information to him about my life, he then began to tell me things about his life. James told me that his wife was divorcing him, and she had moved to New Jersey. I knew he was up to something. The only reason he would have given me that information was that he wanted me know for future reference. I knew his thoughts were impure and that he was trying to make a move.

Innocent enough we carried a conversation and after about an hour I asked him to leave. After that he began showing up more often. I know I should have told him how uncomfortable I was, but I didn't have the courage to speak up. I thought since I was a little distant and had little to say in conversation that he would catch on to the clues, but he didn't.

During this time Jonathan had been calling and checking up on me and my son. He hadn't gotten over what happened in California, but he still cared about our wellbeing. Conversations between him and I became more frequent and less argumentative. I apologized several times and asked for his forgiveness. Over time he forgave me, but never changed his mind about ending the marriage. I made several attempts to make things work between Jonathan and I, but I had cause too much damage for him to ever be able to trust me again.

Jonathan never shared much of what was going on in his life, but I was very curious. One night I had the idea to log into his email and see if I could find out what had been going on with him. As I attempted to log into his account I realized his password had been changed. This made me even more curious. I clicked the 'I forgot my password' link and answered a few security questions and changed his password on my own, but I wasn't prepared for what came next.

I didn't expect to find emails between Jonathan and another woman discussing our soon to be divorce and their upcoming relationship. I was Jonathan's first and was supposed to have been his only. It never occurred to me that Jonathan would move on. I didn't know what to do after reading the many emails between the two of them. I held out hope that after I got my life together Jonathan would come back to me, but at that moment any hope I had dissipated.

As I laid across the sofa with tears running down my cheeks there was a knock at the door. "Come in James." I said. It was as if he heard my tears from across the street. I escorted him in as I normally did and seated him in front of the same window. This conversation seemed to be different this time. I was upset and at this point didn't see any reason to be as private as I had been in the past. A few minutes of conversations turned into a few hours of conversation about my personal and intimate life.

Time was winding down and James got up to leave for the evening. I walked him to the door to say goodbye and as we approached the door James turned to look at me. There was a slight hesitation before he leaned forward and kissed me. What is he doing I thought to myself. I pushed away to let him know that his actions were inappropriate, but before I could speak he told me how beautiful I was.

I began to think about the emails I had read between Jonathan and this other woman. Why not? I asked myself. Jonathan wasn't thinking of me anymore. He had someone else in his life. James didn't seem so bad after that. He slowly let go of the door and the affair between James and I began.

I wish I could say this was the only night James and I had together, but his visits became a regular event. Eventually, late night visits turned into early morning arrivals and mid-day rendezvous. It was all about fulfillment and no attachments for both James and I.

During Church on Sundays, James and I kept our distance from one another. Every so often we would glimpse at each other through our peripheral view. It became very awkward in public, but very relaxed behind closed doors. With each visit it became harder and harder to worship in Church. Soon I just came to punch my ticket as I had done when I was with

Kendrick. I knew eventually I had to stop the affair, but how and when was always the question. All I could think about is what if this became a catastrophe like Kendrick. One thing I did realize is that James was no Kendrick. James was just a body to be had at the moment.

Six weeks after James and I became intimate, his wife returned from New Jersey. James told me about his wife coming home, but had not intentions of ending the affair. James used his work out sessions as his excuse to leave home to be with me. I was curious why he snuck around with me if he and his wife were getting a divorce, but I tried not to think about it.

It was a risk having an affair at my apartment when his wife was just across the street, but the sneaking made the affair exciting. I began to think of the gossip sessions I heard when the old ladies at Church were talking and it became apparent that the gossip was true. James and his wife weren't separated, but could not imagine James had been stupid enough to have an affair with the neighbor that lived across the street. That would have been a recipe for suicide.

The next time James visited I was determined to just talk to him. When he arrived I sat him in the same seat in front of the same window as I sat across from him. Only this time he was very adamant about closing the curtains. I refused and he sat uneasy as I spoke to him about the things on my mind.

"Mr. Washington, I'm pregnant." I said to him. James couldn't believe it. He jumped up out of his chair and immediately questioned the validity of my pregnancy. I sat and said nothing as smoke and fire blew through his ears and nostrils. We began to argue and the argument became very intense. When the smoke cleared the air, I asked him to leave. James left that evening furious with me as if it was my fault I became pregnant. It was finally over I thought to myself. With or without him it was over.

The very next day, around five in the morning, I got up to get ready for work. Suddenly, there was a knock at the front door. Who could be knocking at my door at five o'clock in the morning? I couldn't imagine. I pulled the curtain back slowly to see who was there, and there stood an average height female, short hair and caramel skin. Without a doubt I knew it was James' wife.

The backslider

A Backslider is defined as someone who lapses into previous undesirable pattern of behavior (sin), or follows their own heart. In other words, the Christian has made a conscious decision to follow their own way rather than following God's way.

Zac Poonen states that when you are not sure of your salvation, it is very easy to get discouraged and to backslide. When Michelle heard this statement, she realized that it was the very thing she was experiencing. As she was trying to get her life together, Michelle doubted that God would forgive her for all the horrible things she had done. She couldn't fathom the belief that God would forgive her for breaking Jonathan's heart, betraying Tracy, Neglecting her son, and lying to the Church.

Michelle returned to Church and kept herself busy so that she would stay out of trouble, but there remained that doubt that lingered. Michelle wanted to believe that God would or did forgive her, but she wasn't sure in her faith.

Therefore, brothers, be all the more diligent to confirm your calling and election, for if you practice these qualities you will never fall.
2 Peter 1:10 (ESV)

Michelle began to question her position in Christ. When you are out in the world fulfilling the desires of your own heart, but at the same time confessing Christ, you must consider your position. Am I really a Christian? Am I really apart of God's family? In 2 Peter 1 He asks us to be diligent in confirming your calling. This is not something to be taken lightly. To know where you are in Christ is to know the very essence of who you are. You must take the time and commune with God and seek out His truth.

Michelle came to the conclusion, that during her times of indiscretions, she was not a Christian. This was a hard fact to realize. This will also be hard for many of you to admit, especially to another person, but you must be honest. You must face the fact that your relationship with God is broken. It does not mean that your confession of salvation was not real, but it does mean that you are not living a life of desired behavior that God has called you to. Remember that Christian means to be like Christ, to resemble him, both in our speech and deeds.

> **No one can serve two masters, for either he will hate the one and love the other, or he will be devoted to the one and despise the other. You cannot serve God and money.**
> **Matthew 6:24 (ESV)**

In Michelle mind, she thought she was devoted to God. She prayed many nights for God to send Jonathan back to her. She knew she had hurt him, but she also knew that God could change his heart to forgive her once more. As soon as she realized that she couldn't have Jonathan back, she went back to adultery. Michelle was an adult throwing a temper tantrum because she didn't get what she wanted. She traded the joy of the Lord for the heartache and pain that came along with her sinfulness.

As Christians we have to realize that when we go before God to ask Him of things, sometimes the answer will be NO. It's not that God does not love you. It is that God knows what is best for you. Whether it is that Jonathan was not what God wanted for Michelle or that she was not what God wanted for Jonathan.

In the book of Hosea, God tells Hosea to go and marry a prostitute. Not only was Hosea to go and marry this prostitute, but he was to have children with her. Later in chapter two, God tells the children of Gomer (the prostitute) to plead with her and tell her to stop prostituting. While reading Hosea Michelle realized that she was Gomer. She prostituted herself as a way of escaping the reality of who she was. She wanted to escape the unhappiness in her life that was inevitable caused by her actions.

> **"On that day she will call me her husband,"**
> **declares the Lord. "She will no longer call me**
> **her master.**
>
> **Hosea 2:16 (GWT)**

Michelle committed adultery against God more than enough times for Him to leave her, but because of His love for His people, God remained. God tells us in Hosea 2:16 that He is our husband. God is married to us. In other words, through sickness and in health He is there. God will never leave us nor forsake us. He has declared that those he has chosen, He will never change his mind about.

Sexual immorality affects many people, but the person it affects the most is you. Sex represents oneness with your spouse. Sex is the joining of man to woman. When you are out in the world with different sexual partners you are joining yourselves to them. When the relationship or one night stand is over you live with the oneness of that person that still lingers around. Why? It is because you joined yourself to them. Take a moment and think about the different partners you've been with. After, the relationship ended, did you find yourself taking on some of the same personalities as that person? Perhaps, the ones you hated about them. This is because the two spirits have intertwined with one another.

> **Flee from sexual immorality. Every other sin a person commits is outside the body, but the sexually immoral person sins against his own body.**
>
> **1 Corinthians 6:15 (ESV)**

As Christians we will sometimes stumble. Sometimes we may even fall, but we have to know that we cannot remain in that position. We must repent, get up and brush ourselves off.

> **"Come back, you rebellious people," declares the LORD. "I'm your husband. I will take you, one from every city and two from every family, and bring you to Zion.**
>
> **Jeremiah 3:14 (GWT)**

God is saying to us COME BACK! If you are in sin, COME BACK! If you are an adulterer, COME BACK! If you are a fornicator, COME BACK! If you are a backslider, COME BACK!

God is Calling

I have been asleep,
But it's time to wake up.
Wake up!
Wake up, Nicole!
God is calling me.
Wait, I forgot how to breathe.
Inhale,
Exhale,
I come to rescue thee.
Stand up and walk child,
But I forgot how to move.
One step,
Two steps,
Three!
I do believe it's happening I see.
It's time to pack all your belongs,
But wait these things don't belong to me.
It's mine,
I died,
Then gave them to thee.
Remember, you didn't have to pay for anything.
I gave it free.
I really don't deserve this.
Maybe it's a dream.
Someone pinch me,
Wake up!
Wake up!
Wake up, Nicole!
God is calling me.
Wait, I have some place to be.

Breath,
Inhale,
Exhale,
Speak to me Lord, speak to me!
I'm waiting on you,
Where have you been?
You were supposed to be following me.
Sorry, I lost my step.
My feet forgot how to move.
Here I am!
Here I am!
Can't you see?
Please, don't forget about me.
Wake up!
Get up!
Inhale,
Exhale,
I must go out into the sun,
Where the sun can shine on me.
No, wait!
The sun is too bright.
Can I close my eyes?
If you do,
You can't see those things that are hindering you.
My eyes are heavy,
I need a nap.
Wake up!
Get up!
Inhale,
Exhale,
Are you ready for the Savior to return?
Knock, Knock

Who's there?
It's me.
It's time to go.
Wake up!
Wake up, Nicole!
Something seems to be bothering me.
Was I just dreaming?
Did I just imagine it all?
There is always a warning before the fall.
Wake up!
Wake up, Nicole!
God is calling me!

CHAPTER EIGHT

The moment had finally come when I had to be face to face with James' wife. I wanted to avoid it as long as I could. I wasn't prepared right at that moment. So, I softly tip towed away from the door as to not allow her to hear me at the door. I walked to the back of the house to my bedroom and continued to get ready for work. Every thirty seconds it seemed she would continue to knock on the front door. She had to eventually give up and go away. So, I waited until she did.

I finally finished fifteen minutes later and I gathered all my belongings and headed out. As soon as I stepped out the front door Mrs. Washington came from around the corner. "Are you Michelle Smith?" she asked. "I am." I replied. She introduced herself as Charlene Washington. I prepared myself for the worst. I didn't know what to expect. I trembled as I reached out to shake her hand and say, "How are you today?" I knew exactly how she was doing. I had no doubt in my mind that she had found out about James and me.

Charlene proceeded to tell me that James told her about the affair between him and me, and that I was pregnant. I stood there, waited and watched for her hand to pull back and slap me, but it never came. She only wanted to confirm that I was pregnant, and see whether or not I was going to have the baby. I stood there stumbling over my words as I confirmed everything she wanted to know. I told her that James asked me to terminate the pregnancy, but I refused to do such a horrific thing.

Charlene was concerned about her daughter knowing any siblings she may have and wanted to make sure that what happened would not interfere with that. Then the most shocking thing ever happened, Charlene hugged my neck and told me she would be in touch. She said good-bye and I got into my car baffled about the event that just took place.

All the way to work I replayed every word that was spoken. I was trying to figure out why Charlene was so calm and not angry. Charlene was a very mature and upright woman. She held James responsible for the affair. This was an issue she needed to work out with her husband.

A few weeks later Charlene knocked on my door again, late in the afternoon this time. I answered the door and invited her in. She sat on one side of the room as I sat in front of the window. The same chair I always made James sit in. James was out coaching a football game and this gave her the opportunity to speak with me without him knowing. James had demanded that she not come speak with me, but she needed to know my side of the story before she could try to move on.

Charlene and I talked for two hours hammering out the details of the affair I had with her husband. She sat there and listened to every word. After I had finished my story she informed me of the story between her and James. James had lied to me about everything. James and his wife had never been separated. Charlene had a very sick friend in New Jersey, and she needed to leave to be with her.

While Charlene was in New Jersey, James and her were discussing having another child. This came as a surprise when she found out that James were having a child with another woman. When Charlene left my house I had a feeling that she believed my side of the story as opposed to what her husband had been telling her.

One Saturday morning Charlene returned a third time. This time she came banging on the door is a massive panic. "Michelle! Michelle, open up!" I ran to the door and opened it and she said, "Grab your son and go, now!" Charlene and James had gotten into a fight and he was acting very crazy. He had told her that he was going to kill me and walked out of the house. When he left home, Charlene went out the back door and ran behind the house and across the street to warn me. Without hesitation, I grabbed my son, snatched up the car keys and ran. I sped out of my drive way as fast as I could and drove frantically to my sister's house a few blocks away.

"Why are you over here in your night clothes?" my sister asked. I told her what happened and she took me to her back bedroom, which faced the street, and we looked out the window to see if he followed me.

As my sister and I sat by the window James passed by in his black sedan many times, watching and waiting on me. I knew I needed to come up with a plan. I couldn't sit at my sister's house putting her and her family in danger. I had decided to leave as soon as he made another pass down the street. James didn't know where my mother lived, therefore I left and found refuge at my mother's home.

I stayed with my mother for two days before I decided to go back home. I was afraid to go back home, but I had created this situation by my actions and couldn't stay in hiding forever. My brother escorted me home and checked to make sure everything was clear. Before leaving, he handed me his cell phone and demanded that I not hesitate to call the police if James showed up.

Night after Night I woke up in fear of someone standing outside my house watching me. I was nervous everywhere I went. I knew that I had to keep my son safe. Fear began to consume me and nothing was ever the same.

Having to deal with James, being pregnant, and listening to all the lies and rumors about me became a lot to handle. James had spread rumors that I raped him. At this time I had never heard of a man being raped before. It amazed me at the number of people that actually believed him. Was it because he a minister and his word was truth, or was it because I was an adulterer? It didn't matter the reason, I was scorned and my reputation ruined once again. I couldn't defend any of the rumors. What I had to say meant nothing to anyone anymore. James had told every rumor possible to deflect the blame from him.

After a while, James started calling me again. He continued begging me to have an abortion. He tried any way he could to persuade me, explaining how it would be in my best interest to abort our child. He believed that if I had an abortion all my problems would go away. I knew better. It wasn't that all my problems would go away, but all of his problems would go away.

Time went by and I became further along in my pregnancy. I scheduled an appointment due to some discomfort I was having. The doctor scheduled me for an ultras sound and found that I was suffering from fibroid tumors. He explained to me that the further I get in my pregnancy the more pain I would experience. "If your pain get too severe we will have to operate." He explained.

I couldn't believe I had to deal with another tragedy during this pregnancy. Surely, what I was already going through was enough. I questioned whether or not I made the right decision not to terminate my pregnancy. I pondered the question many times. I knew I couldn't have an abortion because of my beliefs, but was that the only reason? Perhaps, the only reason I should have needed.

The doctor ordered me to bed rest and to sustain for sexual activity, as it would increase my pain level, for the remainder of my pregnancy. This would prove to be a difficult task for me. I had a son at home that I needed to take care of. I tried to view the turn of events as a blessing. If I could sustain from sexual activity during the remainder of the pregnancy, then I would have no problem continuing after the pregnancy. What seemed to be a bad thing would be used to strengthen my walk with Christ.

With everything that was going on I lost my job. While I was looking for new employment I took the time to go back to school, school kept me really busy. I started feeling better about life and developed a self confidence that I lost.

I received a call from Kendrick a few months later asking if he could visit. Now Kendrick didn't know I was pregnant nor did I want him to find out. The relationship between him and I had ended. I told Kendrick I couldn't see him, but he didn't take me serious. A few days later he knocked on the door around midnight. I immediately thought it was James. I quickly rose up and grabbed the knife that I kept under my pillow, and slowly creeped to the door. When I approached the door I saw Kendrick standing there with a big smile on his face.

I open the door and the first thing he notices is my pregnancy. He asked if he could come in and I obliged with hesitation. He entered and sat on the living room sofa exhausted from the tiresome plane ride from California to Atlanta, and then he decided to drive four hours from Atlanta to Lexington, Tennessee. "Why are you here Kendrick?" I asked. "Didn't I tell you not to come?" He thought that once I saw him I would be happy that he was there. Unfortunately, my mind was made up and I didn't want him there.

I asked him to leave, but he sat there on the sofa and didn't move. I then threatened to call the police, but he didn't take me serious at all. For whatever reason, Kendrick never took me serious. He believed my "no" meant "yes", but he would soon find out I meant it when I told him I didn't want him to come.

Finally, I picked up the phone and began to dial 911. He then rose up quickly from the sofa and asked me to allow him to rest overnight and that he would get up in the morning and drive to Dallas to his mother's house. I showed no compassion and demanded he leave right away. I was finally doing better in my life and I didn't want him or anyone else coming in to come in between that.

It was a week before final exams and I went into labor. This was a bitter sweet moment for me. I would no longer have the complications of pregnancy, but I knew I would have to deal with James again. My new son was the most beautiful baby boy I had ever seen. I couldn't imagine anything so beautiful being a part of me. I couldn't believe God had blessed me with such beauty in my life.

James didn't bother visiting us at the hospital nor did he attempt to call. The first thing I knew I had to do was to discredit all the rumors James had spread about me. I filed for child support and along with those proceedings came a Paternity test. It gave me joy to know that the truth would finally be told. In all of my excitement, James began to panic. He knew that the truth would finally come out and he would have to face the truth.

Things in Lexington became tougher for me after giving birth. I struggle emotionally adapting to my son. The physical and emotional stress I went through with James had finally taken its toll on me and manifested itself into Post-Partum Depression. It did not seem to affect the behavior I had with my oldest son, but things were different with my baby.

I was unable to care for him as a mother should. I would hear him cry and could not find the strength to get up and see about him. There were times during breast feeding that I would no longer feed him. I couldn't distinguish for a long time if my behavior stemmed from the fact that my baby looked so much like his father, whom I wanted nothing to do with, or was it truly the Post-Partum Depression. I felt awful as a mother not caring for my child, but it was as if I had no control.

After a couple of days my sister came and took him home with her. She didn't understand the emotional turmoil that I was experiencing, but just thought I needed to rest. I spent the next few days with my oldest son as if he was my only child again. Things had finally seemed normal, except all the baby items around the house. I tried not to allow this to affect me and continued on.

I began searching for a job for weeks later, but was unsuccessful. I had money coming in from school, but it was not enough to cover all the responsibilities that came along with another child. All I could do was pray. I spent days in my house praying and asking God to make a way for me. What right did I have to ask God for anything, but I knew that it was God that had blessed me with this family and it would be God that would help me take care of it.

I went before God and asked Him to forgive me for all my indiscretions. I cried out for Him to deliver me. I couldn't continue on doing the same things I had always been doing. Enough was enough and I was ready to change my life, for real this time. I needed my heart to be changed. God answered me and a life changing experience took place.

Deliverance

Deliverance is the action of being rescued or set free. Michelle needed God's deliverance from the sin of adultery. No matter how many times she tried to walk away on her own, she couldn't do without God. We have been told throughout history that we had the power to rescue ourselves from the grips of the enemy. Michelle had to realize that the enemy was once an angel of God, and God made man lower than the angels. It is not through our power that we can be delivered, but through the power of God.

There comes a time in every Christian's life where they've had a life changing experience. This experience is only given from God himself. This is the moment when God opens your eyes to who you really are and you fall on your face asking God to forgive you and deliver you from your sinful life.

**When the righteous cry for help, the Lord hears
and delivers them out of all their troubles.**
Psalms 34:17 (ESV)

If you are in sin and continue finding yourself going back, it is that you are not seeking the power of God. God says to cry out to Him for help and He will hear you and deliver you from you trouble (self).

**Then they cried to the Lord in their trouble, and
He delivered them from their distress.**
Psalms 107:6 (ESV)

There are some of you that have experienced God's deliverance and there are some that may need His deliverance now. Some may need deliverance from greed, fornication, lying, stealing, gossiping, complacency, procrastination, idolatry, and the list can goes on. Michelle's sin happened to be adultery. Whatever your sin is that you need deliverance from, neither great nor small, cry out to the Lord and He will hear you.

God is faithful in all his dealings with man. Even when we are unfaithful, yet God remains faithful. God saved Michelle from many tragedies that could have occurred during her time of adultery. God kept her from AIDS, HIV, and all other sexual transmitted diseases. He kept her from the rage of Kendrick and James' wives. God kept her children. Not only is God a deliverer, but He is a keeper also. When God has chosen you as one of His own, there is nothing you can do that would cause God to change His mind about you.

> **Know therefore that the Lord your God is God, the faithful God who keeps covenant and steadfast love with those who love him and keep his commandments, to a thousand generations,**
> **Deuteronomy 7:9 (ESV)**

In the book of Judges we see Israel continuous cycle of sin. Israel would turn away from God, God will punish Israel, Israel would cry out to God, and God would deliver them. Israel cycle of sin is not a reason to continue in our sin. Instead, we must learn from Israel mistakes. God is moved by the cries of His people, but Christians often take advantage of God's kindness toward his people. God will deliver you, but he will punish you for your sin.

> **Do not be deceived: God is not mocked, for whatever one sows, that will he also reap.**
> **Galatians 6:7 (ESV)**

Not long after God would deliver the Israelites they would turn away from Him again. When we do not receive what we want from God, when we want it, we turn our backs on Him again. The enemy has tricked us in believing that God is not capable of doing what we ask. When we seek God, we find that the world cannot give us what we are searching for.

A person with a true heart of repentance turns from their sins and began to exhibit Godly behavior. When you're struggling with things, and decide to seek out help from a counselor, the first thing they want to do is get to the root cause of the behavior. Often times we want to point the blame toward others, but there comes a time when we have to examine ourselves. That time is right now.

In the fourth chapter of the book of Ephesians, Paul reference the actions of a thief and how this thief must turn from his sinful behavior and began positive production in his life. There is a root cause of the thief's behavior, which is in verse twenty-eight. The thief is lazy (don't want to work) and he is greedy (not wanting to share). When you get to the root cause you can then began to heal. There was also a root cause in Michelle's behavior. Just like the thief she was greedy. She wanted revenge, and revenge turned into greed. Michelle was never satisfied with what she had. There was nothing wrong with her marriage, but she thought that there was always something more out there and she wanted it.

If we are faithless, He remains faithful-for He cannot deny Himself.
2 Timothy 2:13 (ESV)

There may be a tugging at your heart right now that is calling you to cry out to God. Listen to the Holy Spirit that dwells in you. God is calling you from your sins. He is waiting for you to cry out to Him. God wants to deliver you from your transgressions. Do not resist the Spirit of God, Give in to the Spirit and watch Him do a work in you.

God created us to be more than our sin. God created us for greatness. Through this greatness God is glorified. We are not our testimonies. Our testimonies are used to help those that are lost, so they may be found. Hold strong to your faith and do not give in to the lies of the enemy. You are who God says you are. Michelle is no longer an adulterer. She has been delivered through Christ Jesus. God delivered her and He will deliver you too.

For those who have been delivered, but are afraid to tell your story, just know that your story can save the life of someone who is hiding from the same sin God delivered you from. Being afraid to tell your testimony is how the enemy keeps you in bondage. Stand up in the face of the enemy and declare you have been delivered. Declare that you are not ashamed of where God has brought you from, but that you look forward to where He is taking you.

> **For I know the plans I have for you, declares the Lord, plans for welfare and not for evil, to give you a future and a hope.**
> **Jeremiah 29:11 (ESV)**

Loving Me

It has finally happened! I can't believe it.
I always wondered what it would be like,
I'm in love!
With who?
With me.

I am of a royal priesthood,
I am from a long line of greatness.
I'm a woman...yes that's me.
I realized who God created me to be.
I am more precious than silver or gold.
I know my value; I know exactly what I'm worth.

Did I forget to mention who my Father is?
Yes, that's right. He's the King.
I'm a Princess and I seek to inherit everything.

I'm waiting on my Prince.
Yep. He's coming from the King.
He has already asked for me, but the
King had to explain a few things.
The King had to shape him and mold
him to be perfect just for me.
But before the King could introduce us,
He had to introduce me to me!

Amen.

ABOUT THE AUTHOR

Nicole Miles is a Native of Thomasville, Alabama. After serving her country in the United States Army, she has settled in Copperas Cove, Texas to raiser her two wonderful children in a Loving Christian home.